Santa Claus

Short Poems of All Things Christmas and Santa

(The Historical Origins and Evolution of the Legendary Christmas)

Albert Mathis

Published By **Jackson Denver**

Albert Mathis

All Rights Reserved

Santa Claus: Short Poems of All Things Christmas and Santa (The Historical Origins and Evolution of the Legendary Christmas)

ISBN 978-1-77485-781-6

No part of this guidebook shall be reproduced in any form without permission in writing from the publisher except in the case of brief quotations embodied in critical articles or reviews.

Legal & Disclaimer

The information contained in this ebook is not designed to replace or take the place of any form of medicine or professional medical advice. The information in this ebook has been provided for educational & entertainment purposes only.

The information contained in this book has been compiled from sources deemed reliable, and it is accurate to the best of the Author's knowledge; however, the Author cannot guarantee its accuracy and validity and cannot be held liable for any errors or omissions. Changes are periodically made to this book. You must consult your doctor or get professional medical advice before using any of the suggested remedies, techniques, or information in this book.

Upon using the information contained in this book, you agree to hold harmless the Author from and against any damages, costs, and expenses, including any legal fees potentially resulting from the application of any of the information provided by this guide. This disclaimer applies to any damages or injury caused by the use and application, whether directly or indirectly, of any advice or information presented, whether for breach of contract, tort, negligence, personal injury, criminal intent, or under any other cause of action.

You agree to accept all risks of using the information presented inside this book. You need to consult a professional medical practitioner in order to ensure you are both able and healthy enough to participate in this program.

Table Of Contents

Introduction _____ 1

Chapter 1: The Myths Behind The Myth _____ 8

Chapter 2: Santa Claus In Medieval Europe _____ 34

Chapter 3: Santa In America _____ 52

Chapter 4: Santa Goes Commercial 69

Chapter 5: Strange Adventures Of The Saint's Body _____ 88

Chapter 6: Dangerous Christmas In Old France _____ 117

Chapter 7: The Christmas Tree In Europe _____ 145

Chapter 8: The Story Of The Three Kings _____ 163

Introduction

Christmas is the most significant day in the calendar of year. Following the dates that highlight the national pride of every nation, like Independence Day in the United States, Victory Day in Russia and Bastille Day in France, it's December 25 that embodies the spirit, the work and the economy of a lot across the planet, and includes numerous non-Christian countries. Since the beginning of time the start of winter is the perfect time for the majority of people to gather for food and drink, dance and gather to beat the drums and relax.

In particular, in the 20th century the days that are close to the holiday have turned into an occasion for big business. The winter time is the strongest stimulant for the economy and is more powerful than any fiscal package , since the family incomes and consumers, their spending, credit and consumption in all the productive sectors are dramatically up. For the United States alone, Christmas sales are expected to bring in 3 trillion dollars.

1804 would be an important year on the path to Christmas. In 1804, an antique dealer known as John Pintard founded the New York Historical Society and the organization was a prominent advocate for St. Nicholas to be the the patron in the City. In the following year, writer Washington Irving published, under an assumed pseudonym, a semi-fictional report about New York. Irving used a lot of poetic license to conjure up myths about the city's founding and, in one of these, the admirer Olaf Van Cortlandt, one of the pioneers in New Amsterdam, has a vision in which St. Nicholas reveals to his the bright future waiting for him in the immense lakes and forests "And the wise man Oloffe had a vision and, it happened that the wonderful St. Nicholas came riding across the tops of the trees in that identical wagon, where he gives the annual presents to the children. He then walked downhill to the place where the heroes of Communipaw had gathered for their final dinner. Then he lit his pipe in front of the fire, and then laid at his table and smoked, and while he smoked the smoke of his pipe rose to the air, and grew like a cloud above. Then Oloffe thought about it and he quickly reached an apex of one of highest trees, and noticed the smoke spread across the entire country. And when he thought about it , he realized that the huge amount of smoke took on a myriad of stunning forms. There in the dim light he could see the shadowed outline of palaces, high spires and domes, each lasting only for a brief moment, it faded away until the entire thing was gone and only the green woods remained. Then, after St. Nicholas was done smoking his pipe, he tied it around his hatband and, while putting his finger on the nose of his friend, gave shocked Van Kortlandt an extremely impressive look. Then, after boarding his cart, he made his way back to the top of the trees and vanished."

The next year The Society requested painter Alexander Anderson to make a painting for their annual dinner on the 6th of December, St. Nicholas Day. Anderson's painting, which is a triptych, depicts St. Nicholas standing with an iron rod, and standing the middle of the honeycomb. To his left is a dog, however other aspects of the story have gone missing.

The right-hand side of the triptych the most fascinating. On top of the picture are two boys, a girl wearing her apron filled with fruits smiling and a boy who has unfulfilled hands wiping away his tears. Below the children's hoods is a chimney, with two stockings across the sides. One is filled with gifts, and the other is filled with thesetles. The scene is topped off by toy soldiers as well as cats at the foot of the chimney. The name Sinterklaas which was a challenge to American kids to say, could eventually transform in to Santa Claus during America. United States. [1]

At the same time two additional literary works came out and shaped Christmas. First, there was an assortment written by Washington Irving, entitled Sketch Book which was published in 1819. The book "not only introduced an insight into American writing the characters Ichabod Crane, and Rip Van Winkle, it also it also sparked a wide fascination with Christmas as a relaxing domestic ritual."[2The next was The Visit of St. Nicholas, a poem for children that was referred to by the title "The night Before Christmas," which was published in 1823 anonymously however it is usually attributable to Clement Clarke Moore, a professor at a university who was also a Biblical scholar. The poem was widely circulated and created a solid picture of Santa Claus in the popular imagination, featuring his sleigh, seven reindeers (each one of them with an individual name) as well as the red nose of his, as well as his trip down chimneys in order to fill the stockings of children with toys. According to legend, Moore was inspired by an excursion to shop in a sleigh. the idea of the character of Santa Claus on the character of a Dutchman who resided in Chelsea.

"So all the way to the house-top the coursers that they flew.

With the sleigh filled with toys with the sleigh full of toys, and St. Nicholas too.

Then it happened in a flash. I heard a rumble from the roof.

The pawing and prancing each hoof.

While I was drawing my hand, I was turning,

The chimney is down St. Nicholas arrived with an unbound.

He was dressed of in fur. From his hair to his feet,

The clothes of his were stained with soot and ashes;

A slew of toys that the boy had tossed over his back

He appeared to be the peddler who had just opened his bag.

His eyes were sparkling! his dimples, how sparkling!

His cheeks were as pretty as roses, his nose the shape of a cherry!

His cheeks were pulled up as bows.

And his beard the chin was as white the snow. ..."

In the meantime, the pivotal moment for the old St. Nicholas who is now Santa Claus began with Christmas Day, December 24th 1881 issue of Harper's Weekly. The artist Thomas Nast gave him his most distinctive appearance for the Christmas issue dressed as an older man sporting a large round stomach and an apron, a thick beard of white with a red-colored nose, a cap and a headdress with mistletoe and a miniature horse on one side, and an axe in your fingers and an adorable little boy hanging on his neck.

Since the beginning, Santa has been known around the world for his charmingly puffed-up appearance and jolly forever. For many people, these two adjectives suffice to invoke his nameand cause them to imagine the image of a grandfather-like round-bellied figure dressed in a fur-trimmed cherry-red outfit as well as carrying candy canes and an endless sack of gifts and adorned by a long silvery-white beard.

Santa Claus is a man with a variety of monikers, including Kris Kringle, Father Christmas, Papai Noel, among other names - and is possibly the most well-known and acknowledged person in the recent past. The majority of pop culture fans trace the origins of Santa's name back to Saint. Nicholas of Myra (as suggested by a different title, "Saint Nick") It is widely believed that Coke created the modern picture of Santa that is adored by all of us in the present. Both of them are only partially accurate since in reality, Santa is a vibrant mix of many characters that appear in the folklore of different countries' stories throughout a range of time.

Chapter 1: The Myths Behind The Myth

"Oh it's so exciting to are able to see"the Wild Hunt ride by...

They'll place Hel-shoes on your feet.

They'll make some ale, and then slaughter some animals.

A naked man could ignite your fire,

Then the flames will rise higher ..." - - Jordsvin "The Wild Hunt Song"

It might be surprising to discover that the Americanized Santa Claus beloved by children all over the world in the present, traces one of his first influence to pagan myths and customs, particularly those attributed to the Norse people of Scandinavia.

Within the ranks of the Norse gods there was Wodin more commonly referred to as Odin who was the supreme god. While he was most often associated with healing and death however, he also had a hand in the battlefields of royalty, war poetry, knowledge, and. In the first place, Wodin was a descendant of the ancient Germanic god of the wind and the deceased, usually connected to a female counterpart named "Freya." According to the legends told by Nordic folklore, Wodin was the father of Thor, Baldur, and Tiw and was described as a deeply spiritual being brimming with wisdom, but notoriously unstable.

Georg von Rosen's 1886 painting of Odin

Wodin was the most prominent character of the old Yule the celebration that occurred in the middle of winter, typically overlapping with Winter Solstice (the shortest day of winter) on the 21st day of December. Much like today's Santa Claus, Wodin was an all-knowing god who was loved and hated by the children of Viking areas, particularly in the time of this holiday, since Wodin brought joy to the good-mannered and inflicted adversity on the unruly.

Contrary to the gentle and friendly Santa But Wodin was not soft nor warm. In fact the chiffon-white beards and the semblance of age were the most physical traits they have in common. The aged-looking Wodin had a tall figure, scrawny and wizened , a little like J.R.R. Tolkien's Gandalf and sporting a thick beard that was braided, and a gnarled , wooden staff that he held in his hands for all time. In the paintings, Wodin's naked figure was concealed in a loose dark blue cloak and his hood that was sombre, draped over an unfilled eye socket. There are other depictions of him sporting an open-brimmed hat, or an elongated black cloth and a snugly-fitted pointed wizard's hat for the exact same reason.

If you dig deeper in the meaning of Wodin at the time of Yule and his connection to his contemporary counterparts become more evident. First of all, Wodin, also referred to as "Jolnir," the master of Yule gave gifts and discipline not on an extravagant red sleigh trimmed with gold, but rather on the rear of his most prized flying stallion. It was a stunning eight-legged beast, he dubbed "Sleipnir." Sleipnir was the son of the infamous god Loki in mare form and Svadilfari was a powerful human horse was believed to be the ancestor to Santa's magical herd of reindeer. Wodin was also believed to be with a pair of talking ravens, named Muninn and Huginn and served as faithful pets as well as spying. Wodin was, as the Vikings believed, was the one who watched each of his subjects all through the year. Upon Yule the person would be given the results of Odin's evaluations. Also Wodin knows whether one's been bad or good, so do your best to be kind to Wodin's cause.

Wodin's trip over the sleepy rooftops of the Norse was the scene of what is now known by the "Wild Ride" which is also known as "Wild Hunt." The feared god was atop Sleipnir and took charge of the spectral procession, with a diverse hunter's entourage made up of gods from other religions as well as ghostly souls and supernatural creatures, such as "sword-maiden Valkyries" fairy sprites, fairies and Elves. In addition to hunting, the crew of eldritch swooped down and scared children and adults walking the streets for many hours.

Children who were respectful however are very excited to seeing Wodin. The children filled into their shoes straws, carrot sticks or any other root vegetable for Sleipnir and set them with care on the fireplace, much like children in the present prepare platters made of fresh baked treats and a glass of milk to welcome their visitor at midnight. The boots stuffed with straw may have inspired the stockings that now hang over fireplaces in the indoor space. Wodin crawled through fire pits and danced through to the chimneys in Nordic longhouses and huts. some say he was just a figment of his imagination.

The next day, kids ran to put on their boots. People who passed the tests of Odin exclaimed with joy, for the straws in the shoes was replaced with a handful of apples, sweets and tiny trinkets, in addition to other prizes. The children who had been snarky took off their shoes, crying because inside them was one peril.

Other elements that are inspired by the cult of Wodin are also visible in the contemporary list of Christmas characters. Wodin was, for example, was known by the name of "Lord of Alfheim," land of the Elves. Jewelry, weapons and other items of magical relics were made in a type of factory that stretched miles beneath the surface of the earth which was run by the creatures of the night. There were also the known as "Yule goats." According to medieval mythology, Thor soared through the skies in a chariot pulled by Donder and Blitzen ("Thunder" and "Lightning") The names of from the seven reindeer who drive Santa's sleigh. In the past, Nordic villagers, channeling the Yule goats, put the ratty clothes, terrifyingly intricate masks, as well as many other terrifying costumes, and according to custom, demanded presents and gifts at their neighbours. In the 19th century did the Yule goat changed into a friendly, gift-giving persona. Today, a lot of Scandinavians make straw ornaments made by hand of Yule goats to the branches of their Christmas trees.

Then it was Yule boar, which is not meant to be mistaken for Yule goats. Wild boars with a crisp exterior that had been roasted in a fire were served on platters to offer offerings to Freyr, the Nordic god, Freyr, the god of prosperity, fertility and sacred Kingship. In exchange for the tasty pork - which was perhaps the first Christmas ham - the people were hoping to receive many blessings over the next year, with many betting on the birth of a baby. The gifts of dried fruit cakes and sweets were also offered to Gods Freya and Frigg along with spirits of their ancestors.

The similarities between Yule and Christmas today aren't finished there. After a lavish Yuletide dinner, the locals went into the woods and orchards of local cider apples. In groups they shuffled from tree to the next, adorning evergreens and apple trees, and chanting holy incantations. Singing and humming - or caroling was believed by many to guarantee a prosperous harvest for the coming year. The neighbors and families were also seated in groups weaving and putting together massive pine boughs wheels, that had a resemblance to the wreaths for Christmas that we see today. These wheels of pine, with having a round shape, a symbol that of their "cyclical character of seasons" were then lit and hurled down the hillsides in an honor to Sol the goddess of the sun.

The celebrations that took place during Yuletide was more chaotic and free-spirited nature in comparison to the Christmas celebrations of nowadays, which are characterized by delicious meals and high-quality time. In the days of Yuletide festivities, the Vikings consumed a variety of various meats, as well as soft, juicy fruits and sip goblet after glass of "jol," or "yule," essentially a type of ale. It is possible to say that the Jol is now substituted with eggnog, which is which is a milk-based drink that is thick and heavy. comprised of rum or brandy as well as a mix of sugar, milk and eggs.

Similarities can also be seen in mythical characters that aren't part of the mythology of Wodin. As we've mentioned the white-bearded, Hammer-wielding Thor often referred to in the form of "Thunor," is believed to be a different mythological creature which influenced contemporary depictions of Santa. The enchanting goats of Thor aside the god was frequently depicted in red-colored royal clothing and, in some drawings depict him sporting an unruly, red-hot ginger. Furthermore the white, red and black that are that Santa's outfits were and robes, perhaps (and possibly not) represented the colors that were associated with the past of Germany and it's Aryan casting system.

Martin Winge's 19th century painting depicting Thor

The 1980s were when some historians claimed to have discovered evidence connecting Santa to the mystical Siberian Shamanism. Jason Mankey of Patheos explained, "In this hypothesis, Santa is a shaman who rides in a sleigh. The reindeer represent Siberian spirits of reindeer and his white and red costume is derived from the agaric fungi used to aid in the trance of shamanism. Shamans, in actuality, didn't ride in sleighs and seldom interacted with reindeer spirits and used the mushrooms only in very limited instances. Furthermore the reindeer was an Nineteenth Century addition to the Santa-mythos, and Siberians did not wear red or white attire. Therefore If Santa is connected to shamanism it's indirect."

the Man Behind the Myth

"Children I implore you to change your heart and your thoughts so that you can be pleasant to God. Remember that while we believe that we are innocent and sometimes be deceived by men, we are able to conceal anything against God." - - attributed to Saint. Nicholas of Myra

Then, Wodin and other pagan cults were essentially wiped out by a new religion that was dominant: Christianity. A growing number of rulers and sovereigns began to embrace the monotheistic faith and, eventually the sacrilegious act worshipping Wodin as well as other gods of pagan origin was declared illegal. In the same vein the ancient customs of Yule were discarded and the holiday was delayed in order to be more in line with Christian celebrations.

A key figure in Christianity will be the most famous of all Santa's ancestors. The 3rd century in the tiny Turkish town in Patara, Nicholas of Myra was both born and embraced by the luxury of the world however, despite his wealth the tragedy struck him because both his mother as well as his father became seriously sick and passed away shortly afterwards.

Of course, Nicholas was deeply saddened by the sudden loss of his parents however, he decided to put his wealth to use. Instead of spending his money in extravagant, but unneeded houses, extravagant clothes and other frivolous items that were not needed, he donated the whole of his wealth to those who were poor and struggling to find relief.

Nicholas was a well-known figure for sure. The most frequently-repeated story about this enchanting character involves him settling the dowries of three girls who were homeless and thereby preventing women from prostitutes. In the evening of the first one of their fathers was instructed to nail an array of stockings (in different versions and other versions, boots) on the wall below one window in their tumbledown hut, according to the ordered by the party who was providing the dowries. Within a couple of minutes after the planned time an enormous pouch of gold flew past the window and ended up in the stockings. The stockings were discovered by the father who was ecstatic the next day. As Nicholas promised, two additional pouches of gold were found in the stockings in the next two evenings. This is a different possible source of the Christmas stocking custom.

A Renaissance painting depicting the father receiving the dowries for his daughters.

An Greek Orthodox icon that depicts St. Nicholas slapping Arius during the First Council of Nicea.

A Russian icon depicting St. Nicholas

The word quickly spreads about the humble but immensely generous and powerful Nicholas He was later made as the bishop of Myra. The memory of him lasted long after his demise, and was revered for being the saint who is regarded as patron saint to children and protector of sailors, orphans and prisoners. The secrecy and modesty that characterized Nicholas his charitable work according to some, was the source of inspiration for the now well-known game, "Secret Santa." In addition, like the observant Santa, Nicholas also urged children to faithfully say their daily prayers and to honor their parents and to practice proper behavior.

There aren't any contemporary accounts or works on St. Nicholas. A biography of a saint in the region which was written about 100 years later, recounts an excursion to the grave of Nicholas of Myra. His name is also mentioned on a list of those who attended of the Council of Nicea, although the list was composed more than one century after the ceremony. Two of the oldest sources to mention the proto-Santa Claus.

In 520, a little over 2 centuries following his demise in 520, a church dedicated his memory was constructed on the remains of an earlier temple in which he was said to have was a bishop. The fact was verified in 2017 through an expert Turkish government excavation that revealed the remains of an old church under the building built in the 6th century. So there is no doubt regarding the existence of an historical St. Nicholas who had tradition of helping the less fortunate and giving gifts in secret regardless of whether the Lives of his life were heavily influenced by mythology. The feast of St. Nicholas was held on the 6th of December and he was designated as the patron saint of children.

It was believed that the ancient Greeks living in Myra in the Lycian village in Myra mourned the passing of their bishop. The kindling they utilized to protect the fiery memories of him was the stories and myths associated with Saint. Nicholas's miracles. They lavished them on merchants who passed by and travellers from the next town. The riveting tales eventually took on the form of their own and so new stories, which were not tested, started to appear in the mix.

Nicholas was initially regarded as the patron of navigation. He was the saint who defeated his Pagan Divine Twins from Myra. Statues depicting the twosome who were the sons of the Sky God were taken down and replaced by beautiful hand-carved effigies of the holy Christian bishop. As time passed, the saint's image was included on the majority of formal Byzantine seals.

The more Greek towns and cities were able to adopt Nicholas to be their patron saints. Doing it was only right since Nicholas was also the patron saint of the Byzantine Empire was encircled in the Mediterranean. When Christianity first entered in the Kievan Rus during the ninth century sailors and sea captains of the region (the first state to be organized within the Russian territories) were also put under Nicholas his protection. It is interesting that - in addition to sailors, orphans and children, the pawnbrokers too chose Nicholas as their patron saint. Three golden balls that heardken back to the three gold pouches that the bishop gave to three sisters, were seen hanging above the doors to the pawn shops.

At the time, people living in Western Europe knew of St. Nicholas, but they did not know the intriguing specifics of his story. The situation changed when the Seljuk Turks descended upon Anatolia in 1071, retaining the momentum gained from winning the Battle of Manzikert against the Emperor Romanus IV Diogenes and the Byzantine forces. The inhabitants of Myra prepared themselves for the inevitable, and accepted their captives.

The year 1087 was when a group comprised of Christian Greeks based in "the the heel of Italy" came up with an idea for "recover" Nicholas's relics of glory of The Muslim conquerors. The following spring, a team disguised as merchants was sent to Myra. Then, following the directions by the merchants, they lowered themselves to the ground, snatched the skeleton, along with a variety of other relics. They then fled in Bari, Italy. The discovery of Nicholas's remains in Mari on the 9th of May is now celebrated by the church as"the "translation of Saint Nicholas." A couple of winters after, after the pope Urban II's opening of the cathedral that was built in Bari Nicholas's remains were placed under the altar of the main.

The saint's remains are in Christian hands, exactly where they belonged, the church sent missionaries to nearby towns, informing those who were unaware of Nicholas the miraculous feats. Bari soldiers who traveled across the globe also carried along the stories of Nicholas's amazing achievements and he soon became the most sought-after saint throughout Europe.

Within the West, Nicholas was extolled as the patron holy saint for all kids. On this day of celebration 6 December Christians revered him by giving gifts to loved family members and friends. This custom was reported to have been observed in Utrecht The Netherlands from as early as 1163.

It is believed that the idea was sparked by a petty group of nuns from an unknown French village. In the beginning, they travelled just to the shacks in disrepair or sleeping spots of homeless children, and then sneakily left small bags of candy before disappearing into the night. When the operation grew the nuns were able to sneak through the doors that were unlocked of empty houses, placing candy bags inside the shoes of good-mannered, and then just a few turns of the willows into the shoes of children who had been troublesome. How they managed to keep track of children who were in trouble is not clear and one could only guess that some sort of cooperation between parents and nuns occurred.

Most of the time the nuns chose to remain unidentified. If asked about the source for these gifts they would only respond: "It must have been St. Nicholas!"

The nuns did not all deliver sweets. In day one of St. Nicholas Day, families in need awoke to a basket of bread and other food items and also boxes of clothes, and sometimes, gold coins, wrapped up in cloths. Sometimes, the nuns put a single tangerine, or apple (a expensive fruit in the past) in the stockings' heels and fill the remainder of the room with a mix of nuts.

The custom of giving out gifts during St. Nicholas Day eventually was adopted by other regions of the Low Countries, spreading to Germany, Austria, Switzerland and England and eventually Romania. In the early days, French nuns were always replaced by the Spirit that was St. Nicholas, painted as a thin wrinkled wraith clad in a bishop's robe of scarlet.

The 13th century was the time when, by the 13th century's end sweets and other foods were discarded in favour of bigger ornaments and other novelties with particular significance. This new phase of giving gifts, as historians speculate that it was inspired from the Catholic Church with the aim of integrating the gifts extended to The Three Magi in the story of the Nativity to the Christmas season. Entrepreneurial vendors tried to profit from the current trend by creating "St. Nicholas markets" where there were colourful stalls that were filled with trinkets and toys and other treats.

European royalty also began to take part in the tradition of gift-giving. The year 1377 was when the courtly subjects of the French monarch Charles V received gilded chalices that were filled to the top with myrrh, incense and gold blocks. At New Year's Day, subjects who were able to afford it gave their monarchs an array of attractive presents. It was a blessing for them that they didn't go home empty-handed as they left the royal chambers with either a silver-gilt bowl or a bag of coins.

While St. Nicholas Day had been a symbol of gifts and generosity however, he was not the happy-go-lucky, rosy-cheeked Santa Claus of 21st Century. Children living in the fervently Catholic areas of Europe was terrified of the advent from the ghostly Saint because he was portrayed as a moral yet vengeful bogeyman that was a snare to wicked children.

In Germany There were two gift-givers bound through an "good cop good cop, bad cop" dynamic: St. Nicholas and his ally, Knecht Ruprecht (Farmhand Rupert). Rupert was dressed in a dirty brown (sometimes white lace) jacket with a hood that was edged with black fur, wandered the streets during the dark of night, saturating his stomach with children who were causing trouble. In Switzerland and in the Netherlands, Nicholas shoved bad children into the void in his sack, with the attention of a litter collection truck outfitted with trash collection device. The pulsing sack full of children was then dumped to the Black Forest, never to be returned to.

In some parts of Austria the religious leaders were even more insistent in driving home the importance of a proper behavior. On the day of his feast the saint, clad in full bishopric regalia knocked on the doors of children who had been snubbed and demanded to be allowed into the home. The children, in a panic, were unable to get in, and hid in mattress or inside closets. After the water was declared clean, they emerged from their hiding places and were snatched and escorted into another room, accompanied by the waiting bishop. The bishop then sat over the children who were crying and flicked the switches with his fist in a swift movement but stopped short of the head of the crying child. When the child reacted in a similar manner the bishop was furious and said he'd be returning the next year. If they were gifts or rod-beatings St. Nicholas always delivered.

Teachers at Christian schools, specifically those who are associated with saints started to carry on the custom. Every year on the 6th of December they would sit at their desks and dressed in the image of the saint of the gods. As one by one students stood up to hear their opinion. Students with excellent or satisfactory grades and excellent conduct were awarded sweets or spending money. Students who had subpar scores and bad conduct were confined to the classroom after dismissal and beat with rods made of birch.

These penalties had become an essential part of St. Nicholas Day traditions However, they were not the only thing that was in place. Roman Catholic Church reminded Christians not to forget the main message of the day. Showing love for one's children and expressing admiration for their behaviour was a good thing but it was far more important for those who were wealthy to give their wealth to the less fortunate. According to Ambrose of Milan and a close associate with St. Nicholas, once stated, "You are not making the gift out of the things you own to a needy. You are giving the person what belongs to him. What has been granted to all for the benefit of all, you've granted to yourself. The world has been made available to all of us and not just to the wealthy."

While the notion of intentionally encouraging children to put their trust in a fictional person might appear a bit odd or outdated to some however, the above evidence suggests that this kind of trickery was not a new phenomenon. As time went on, devious parents throughout Europe continued to maintain the pretenseand were able to modernize the earlier customs of St. Nicholas Day. The 15th century Swiss writer, Rudolf Hospinian, noted, ""It was the custom to parents during the night of the saint Nicholas to give secret gifts of all kinds to their children and daughters, who were instructed to believe they owed the generosity that was shown by St. Nicholas as well as his train. The train traveled between towns and villages, would stop into the windows, even though they were closed and gave them away."

The same sentiment is present in a poem written by the 16th century German dramatist Thomas Naogeorgus:

"...And whenever they all one in the late at night

The slumbers of the night are tangled

The apples, nuts and pears,

There are other things that go along with it.

In the form of caps, and shoes, as well as petticoats and shoes

In secret, they cover up,

Then in the early morning, they found the following:

This St. Nicholas brought ..."

The popularity in the St. Nicholas-inspired gift-giving trend was waning in 1517, marking the dawn of the Protestant Reformation. Catholics were repeatedly scolded by the church for "undue" reverence for the canonized, particularly towards the miracle guru St. Nicholas. It was the Industrial Revolution, the rise of Puritanism in Europe and opposition to the veneration of saints, that included particular celebrations for St. Nicholas and St. Wenceslaus, overshadowed the celebrations in Europe. It was the Calvinist religious theologian Walich Sieuwertz wrotethat "It is an unwise and ineffective practice to fill the shoes of children with all kinds of sweets and other nonsense. What is more sinister than the sacrifice of an idol? The people who perform it don't know what religion actually is." According to Their History of New York, Edwin Burrows and Mike Wallace note the following "since the Reformation protestants have rejected Christmas as a result of Catholic insanity and deceit. The New Testament silent on the day of Christ's birth they remarked, but the Church had chosen the 25th of December to be the day that marked the beginning of the winter solstice. which was a time typically connected with wild, pious bacchanals as well as opposition to the authority of."

Martin Luther, the seminal leader of the Reformation was the first to ban any celebrations honoring saints in Protestant regions. However, Luther had no delusions about the law which he was enforcing and he was aware of the unwelcome celebrations that were bound to occur out of view. In an attempt to fill in the gap left by an ecstatic figure in winter, Luther spun together the story of Christkindlein.

Christkindlein also called "Christkindl," or simply "Christkind," directly translates to "Christ Child." Initially Christkindl was depicted as an adorable, cherub-like Jesus in the form of a toddler. German Christians, however, did not buy the notion of a small or wings-like Christ flying between houses in the winter months as no story or reference to a gift-giving Christ is found within the Gospel. To correct this, a new figure was created. In the future, Christkindl was no longer Christ but rather an androgynous and nameless baby angel sporting butterscotch-blonde rings, sparkling blue eyes and golden, fluffy wings.

The imagery of Christkindl varied across different parts of Protestant Europe that included areas that are today Austria, Liechtenstein, Hungary, Switzerland, Slovakia, and the Czech Republic. In certain versions, Christkindl was depicted as a girl with no wings dressed in a hooded fur coat, walking through thick sheets of snow. Sometimes, a deer was seen jogging alongside her, carrying a large basket of toys and fruit resting upon his hind snout. At other times, Christkindl completed the task alone, pushing her wheelbarrow full of toys through the snow's curtain of falling.

Christkindl was not born on the 6th December, but on 24th day of the month and the final day of the Advent. Presents were neatly placed under the Weihnachtsbaum which was an evergreen tree that was decorated with lighted candles, which is now considered to be as the precursor to the tree for Christmas. In the customary period, Protestant parents advised their children to not get Christkindl. the angel of gifts was said to have escaped the homes of curious young youngsters. It was only when they heard the sound from the bell (hooked to the bell with their parent's permission) did they rush from their rooms and make a run to the gift beneath the Weihnachtsbaum.

Another legend, however, is that it attributed the creation of the Christmas tree, or its "Christianization" of the Yule log according to Martin Luther, who was supposed to be walking through the snowy forest on Christmas Eve. He spotted the gorgeous light shining off the branches on a fir and was so touched that he brought one to his house to convey to his son the true Christmas message the fact that Christ was the Christ who was the light of the world. The story's origins are unmistakably mythological tale could be the work of an artist called C.A. Schwerdgeburth that depicts the founder for the Reformation and his family around a gorgeous Christmas tree.

Chapter 2: Santa Claus In Medieval Europe

"Each of you should contribute what you've chosen to give, and not unwillingly or in the face of pressure, because God is fond of a cheerful giver." 2 Corinthians 9:7

Numerous variants in the name of St. Nicholas continued to be discovered throughout Europe throughout the years that followed.

The 16th-century English diary writer Henry Machyn recounted the enthralling St. Nicholas Day celebrations which took place in the city streets in London around 1550. "[People dressed in Nicholas the bishop's costumes] traveled around in many parts of London singing in the traditional fashion...received by good-hearted people into their own robes and were able to enjoy as lots of cheers like they did throughout the city. ..."

Incredibly, although the words "Father Christmas" and "Santa Claus" can be interchanged within the United Kingdom today, the first Father Christmas and St. Nicholas were not the identical. The unnamed forerunner of Father Christmas (named as

Grandfather Christmas to avoid to create confusion) made his debut in pagan mythology and customs of mid-winter time of the early British people.

Contrary to what his name may suggest the"King Frost was the herald of springtime. He was a massive white-bearded, white-bearded figure swathe the length of a floor-length cloak in emerald green decorated with a single wreath of ivy and holly or mistletoe. The moment that Britain began to enter the Anglo-Saxon era during the fifth century CE the role that was Grandfather Christmas was combined with the character of "Saxon Father Time," also known as "King Frost," or "King Winter." Dawn Copeman of Time Travel Britain explained, "Someone dressed in the role of King Winter to be invited into homes, where they would be seated by the fireplace and be served food and drinks. It was believed that by being nice to King Winter people would be rewarded with something positive in return, namely a less harsh winter. So, Father Christmas became associated with receiving gifts of good quality."

The last elements that would make up this medieval Father Christmas was the advent of the Normans which brought along the legends of the mythical St. Nicholas.

The first mention of Father Christmas, however, dates back to the 15th century. composed by the Rector from Plymtree, Richard Smart:

"Nowell, Nowell, Nowell, Nowell,

"Who is the one who sings like that?

"I am here I am here, Sir Christemas.'

'Welcome, my lord Christemas,

Welcoming to all of us More or less

"Come near, Nowell! '"

It was then it was that Father Christmas became the embodiment of the Christmas spirit. In the Tudor and Stuart period, Father, Sir, and Captain Christmases were invited to parties in the winter months and Christmas display events held by public establishments as well as in the grand salons of the upper classes.

In 1638, the Worcestershire-born dramatist Thomas Nabbes produced the first picture that synthesized Father Christmas in his court costume, The Springs Glorie: A disheveled, rotund and pipe-smoking man, with tiny eyes that were smiling, whisker and beard that resembles the color of freshly fallen snow, attired in the traditional "furr'd cap and gown." The night before Christmas, Father Christmas galloped all across the city with his donkey, or his horse with small presents he slipped into pillowcases and stockings, and hanging over the fireplace or the headboards of children's beds. In a gesture of gratitude, children cooked for Father Christmas a slice of mince pie, served with the brandy in a tumbler.

Unfortunately, by the middle of the seventeenth century ultra-conservative English Puritans who couldn't endure the excess and the intoxicant drinking associated with Christmas prohibited the Christmas season - and Father Christmas - altogether. But, the faithful still paid tribute for Father Christmas while taking their activities underground. The character was seamlessly incorporated into wintertime Mummers' plays ("seasonal folk-based plays performed by a group of actors known by the name of "mummers" (or "guisers"). The following is an opening phrase commonly used in these productions: "In comes I, old Father Christmas," the actor declared as he entered the stage. "Be I welcomed or am I not? I'm hoping that an old Father Christmas will never be lost."

Apart from these cult TV shows, Father Christmas also made appearances in newspaper back-alley articles. The writers of the newspaper that were in question refer to Father Christmas in the form of "Old Christmas,"" that was a symbol of the nation's resentment towards the holiday they were forbidden to celebrate. Pamphlets written by fans and also called "recusant Catholics" on the explicitly demanded an upcoming return to Father Christmas. The following passage is from one of the pamphlets "Any man or woman who can share any information or share any news of an old gray-bearded, very old man, known as Christmas, who was believed to be a frequent guest and visited all kinds of people, rich and poor and was often seen in sparkling silver, silk and gold and in court and in all forms in the theater of White Hall, and had bells ringing, feasts, and joy everywhere as well as in the city and out in the country in anticipation of his return - anyone who can discern what has the fate of him or where he could be and when he will be back into England!"

The ban of Father Christmas was eventually lifted but it wasn't until at the point that Britain was entering in the Victorian Age that the Christmas spirit returned at full speed.

While 323 miles away further east from London, Dutch children across the Netherlands were waiting patiently for the arrival of Sinterklaas. The 17th century saw trees were the norm across northern Europe. Unidentified 35-year-old who was in Strasbourg in 1605 recorded the following description within his journal of travel: "At Christmas time in Strasbourg people would put up the fir trees in their living spaces. They then hang roses cut into papers of a variety of colors, 40 apples wafers, and goldplated (decorations). "[4However that this doesn't suggest that people were putting pine trees in the center of a living space. In some areas in Austria and Germany the tree was placed upside down in the area in the corner and decorated with walnuts, apples and pieces of paper with colors. Other were just large branches that were hung from doors and windows. There was at most an entire century before the symbol would take its current form.

At this point historians also can trace some of the first references to Sinterklaas throughout Europe which is a combination from St. Nicholas, Father Winter and perhaps Odin. It's not entirely clear when the Christian bishop became a winter figure and possibly Sinterklaas, the Norse god, but the majority of the elements in the myth of Sinterklaas appear to be out of any Christian traditions, not to mention how saints developed fantastical traits in those in the Middle Ages. According to legend Sinterklaas flies across the sky on a horse , accompanied by a group of demon-like or black assisters who instruct him on human behaviour. There are other stories that claim Sinterklaas is seen in villages, accompanied by a dark assistant known as Zwarte Piet (Black Pete), a villainous character who imposed corporal punishments to children or abducted children to transport their bodies to an area where they would suffer.

A drawing of Sinterklaas and Black Pete

The night of December 5, Dutch children pored over Scripture for hours before the arrival of Sinterklaas as the reason for his trip was to instruct the children on their biblical understanding. It was vital to pass the test in a breeze failing which would mean the permanent sacrificial death of their souls.

Five minutes prior to arriving at Sinterklaas The children of the household gathered in an orderly line in front of at the entrance to the house. After a short hymn that praised the saint for his unmatched kindness the door was smashed open. A sluggish hand stepped in through the gap in the door and threw a few sweets into the hallway. And then, without warning, the door opened and then in came Sinterklaas typically played by a parentor friend, or neighbour.

The angry Sinterklaas entered the hall and walked around the children, the red cape that he was wearing over his bishop's white alb flying behind the swathe of red. After a long pause of jittery children, they were instructed to sit down on chairs each. Then, he went back and forth the middle of them, striking a birch rod into an open palm while the children were asked questions on different sections from the Bible.

"Who did not obey God and in the process transformed into a salt pillar?"

"What is the sea on which Moses make a part of?"

"Recite the 10 Commandments!"

For every correct answer, children were awarded a second round of sweets (and sometimes even oranges). However, every mistake was greeted with a fervent punishment of a smack on the wrist or child's back. Children who couldn't come up with a single correct answer were sentenced to eternity in the fiery deeps of Hell. Children who failed for two years consecutively were put into Sinterklaas dirty sacks and then dragged away to Lucifer's abode.

Spanish Aragon took over Bari and the remaining areas of the Norman Kingdom of the Two Sicilies 1442. Holland did the same after which it decided to be absorbed into the Kingdom of the Spanish Hapsburgs 100 years after. After the change, Dutch Catholic bishops began to travel to Spain as well as the spirit of St. Nicholas, they claimed, traveled through the lush Spanish countryside along with the bishops. In the beginning there was a major hurdle that prevented Sinterklaas from disengaged from his duties. He was unable to not keep his eyes of the Dutch children in order to ensure that his log of behavior was up-to-date and accurate. This is why Sinterklaas hired an untrained Moorish man known as Zwart Piet (Black Pete) and tasked with observing the children as well as updating the record during his absence. In the following years, Zwart Piet began to accompany Sinterklaas when he went on gift-giving excursions with his own bag the birch rods to give to the naughty and ungodly children.

Anthropology Professor Benjamin K. Swartz, Jr. explained the Black Pete's character Black Pete in further detail: "In function, Black Pete functions as an Dutch non-pagan counterpart to Knecht Ruprecht, the German Knecht Ruprecht (Farmhand Rupert)...a black sprite who assists St. Nicholas as a discipliner or child. Ruprecht is seen in a shaggy carrying a sack over his back...and rod in his hand' during the sixteenth and seventeenth centuries...The English counterpart of Knecht

Ruprecht, Robin goodfellow is known from 1489 and he was known for his high-pitched scream of Ho Ho Ho. In actual fact, many supernatural "little ones" were linked to St. Nicholas during the time of his appearance within German folklore, resulting in his eventual status as an elfin and his collaboration with the elf-helpers."

19th century Swedes using a chapter from the work of British Christians in the 1550s went out in the streets to show off extravagant and vividly-colored parades that aimed to enliven the Christmas spirit. Court servants and court subjects from the royal retinue of the king Oscar II - with some faces were covered in stage makeup and others hid in intricately detailed masks performed Christmas songs and carried their gifts baskets in their arms. The impressive variety of costumes was endless that included royals and soldiers, sailors, and scary Harlequins. The main character of the Swedish tradition of giving gifts was Julbocken the "Christmas goat" that first came into the public sphere through Petter and Lottas Jul (Peter and Lotta's Christmas) which was written by writer Elsa Beskow. The magical goat, likely a derivative of Knecht Ruprecht was presented as a mythical figure who gave presents and gladness to kids who were well-behaved.

The Tomten was a second prominent figure of the pantheon. Tomtens were small and tubby gnomes-like creatures sporting beards of curly white hair as well as pointed, red capes. They resided in the crawlspaces of every Swedish house, securing the children and all animals in the area against evil spirits as well as other negative energies. In mid-December, the tomtens moved to the attic as well as the hollow space under stairs, as well as other corners and crevices within the home. After all the members of the family were snuggled in their beds, the curious gnomes burst out of their hiding spots and dumped unintentionally discarded treats and valuable trinkets inside difficult-to-find spaces creating an unending search for treasures to be found by the whole family.

If the family triggered the tomten they would retaliate. The family would later be the target of small, but gruesome jokes (i.e. socks that are missing or gloves, toys or the early deflation of milk) as well as be cursed with a string of luck.

In the 1800s, two characters had been merged into one person: the Jultomten also referred to as Tomten or Nisse. Jultomten was a tough non-fussy shape-shifter who took on the shape of a short, crooked-backed , gentleman dressed wearing a long worn-out coat. The gift basket he carried was placed in the back of the ram. The night before Christmas, the Jultomten banged at every front door. "Have the children in there been ok?" he boomed from the opposite part of the front door. When Jultomten was informed by the household's parents the family, he swiftly walked through the front door and handed over the gifts, apparently scurrying through the door within the quickness of a blink.

To show their appreciation To express their gratitude, children made porridge bowls with savory ingredients and platters of butter and almonds and left them in the main entrances to their home. Jultomten could also be paid for with a gift of alcohol or tobacco. Anyone who did not take this step were at risk of being punished by the generous gift-giver who was pint-sized. In addition to receiving the cold shoulder of the Jultomten the next year, they were also subjected to cruel tricks and petty jokes.

Furthermore In Sweden and a few parts of Germany there was a trend exchanging gifts that they called "Yule-klapp" to show a form of thanksgiving towards St. Nicholas. Yule-klapp were usually chains, pendants, necklaces adorned by precious stones or other sparkling gift. They were wrapped in silk and packed in multiple boxes that increased in size giving an Russian nesting doll appearance. According to custom, the presenter approached the door of the home of the recipient, and when the person who received the gift came to meet them, the gift-giver throws the Yule-klapp over the door before escaping as fast as their legs could take the presents, in order to conceal their identity.

The mixing between St. Nicholas and Christmas customs has led to more delightful customs. The tradition in France, Pere Noel (the French version to St. Nicholas) was presented as a slim aged man in a loose, hooded red robe, trimmed with white fur. His gifts were not carried through a sack rather, a hotte, which was a hand-woven basket that resembled those used by the grape harvesters. On December 24, French children dusted off their boots and sabots (clogs made of wood) and filled them up with apple slices and carrots for the donkey of Pere Noel, Gui and laid them on the fireside. To celebrate Pere Noel they made glasses of fine wine or Calvados which is one of the varieties of apple or pear brandy made by the Normandy region of France.

Contrary to popular belief the mythical gift-giver wasn't always a male character. Consider the example of Lady Befana of Italian legend. In the time that the Three Wise Men ventured out from the Middle East in search of the new king they were relying on the Star of Bethlehem as their guide. The long journey they took traversed a variety of cities and nations, including among them was an unmarked and secluded village in Italy. Every village they encountered rushed into the crowds in order in order to take them on their way to where they wanted. The moment the magnetic Magi came by in the Italian village, the entire inhabitants swarmed into the streets and followed in a masse, joining the cortege of wise men that was rapidly growing with the exception of one tiny old lady.

"Come fast!" her neighbors called out to her. "The Three Magi are here!"

"Do not be patient with my return," the old lady responded, before sweeping them away using her broom. "There is a lot of housework to be completed however I am in no doubt I'll be done before you leave."

The lady worked around her house, mopping scrubbering, cleaning, and scrubbing while ignoring the fading and rising sun. When she was done with her housework, she laid her broom down and cleaned her hands over the sides of her rough dress, admiring the cleanliness of her work. Then she took notice of the striking silence, the pin-drop silence and the the early morning sun kissing her cheek. The lady grabbed the present on the table for dinner and walked out the doorwith her with her broom in her hand and the villagers long gone.

La Befana La Befana, as she has been named but has not yet completed her quest to become the new King. Every year on the 6th January, she climbs aboard her broomstick to fly across the world and stops at the homes of each child along the journey. She pulls one of the gifts from her bag, that she wears as an actual backpack, and then swoops through the fireplace, placing an assortment of gifts into hand-knitted stockings , or placing them on the christmas tree. Unable to find the king's newborn and her king, she presents a gift to each child in the hope that she will be able to locate the king.

The story about Befana was first discovered during the period of 13th-century, kids were instructed to remain in their bed. Anyone who disobeyed the instructions of their parents as it was said they were hit hard on the back of their heads by her broomstick. To show their gratitude to Befana for her trouble the entire family assembled an assortment of sandwiches and other finger foods, and accompanied them with the glass or two of red wine.

Italian kids spent the final week of December making stockings, writing lists of wishes and letters to Befana about their actions throughout the year. The children who were well-mannered could find beautiful dolls, handmade puppets and wooden novelty items within their stocks. The children who were not so well-behaved however received stockings that were filled with coal, garlic, and old onions bulbs.

Chapter 3: Santa In America

"Santa Claus" is a person who cares about another and tries to please them and gives his heart by the thought, word, or action in each gift Santa gives and shares his joy with people who are sad; whose hands are never closed to the needy...who acknowledges a friend and brother in every person who he meets on his regular road. ..." Edwin Osgood Grover 1912

St. Nicholas' winged horse first came to New York in the New World in the early 17th century, along with the Dutch as well as German colonists who chose to establish themselves on the continent of North America. The records are scant however, historians believe the traditions of giving gifts to Saint Nicholas' benevolent patron saint were initially followed in Dutch families, mostly located in New Amsterdam (now New York City). German, Belgian, and Polish colonists who were stationed in Pennsylvania might have also celebrated the feast to St. Nicholas.

On the 23rd day of December, 1773, English-born James Rivington's New York Gazetteer published an article about the Boston Tea

Party. In the article, he noted the fact that families of Dutch families had met in a local tavern for a celebration to celebrate St. Nicholas: "Last Monday, the anniversary of St. Nicholas, otherwise known as St. A Claus, was observed in Protestant Hall, at Mr. Waldron's house. A large number members of the family of this old saint celebrated the day with excitement and celebration." Rivington was, so, the first person to write an item within North America that mentioned St. Nicholas and his feast day with the proper name. It is evident that Rivington also made the very first mention of "Santa Claus," identifying the man as "St. The Claus," possibly a mispelling from "Sinterklaas," the Dutch "Sinterklaas."

St. Nicholas was omitted from the pages of his papers and was not recorded until about 20 years later. This is when his traditions were revived by an New Yorker by the name of John Pintard. Pintard is a businessman who was also a philanthropist, active Freemason and secretary for the Academy of Fine Arts - expressed his fascination with St. Nicholas in his private journal between 1793 and 1797. However, it wasn't until the early years in the late 19th century when he decided to keep his actions off of the paper.

Pintard

In 1804 Pintard was one of the eleven founders of the New York Historical Society, believed to be the very first museum in the state. Pintard was aware of the importance of keeping and preserving journals as well as books, eyewitness account books as well as other documentation of their lives, thus rescuing the records from "dust and disgrace." The skepticism of these men was strengthened through what they had experienced during those years of the American Revolution and the British invasion of New York City in 1776. They long for simpler times and were horrified at the immorality and lack of godliness that seemed to be the norm for New York norms.

St. Nicholas was unofficially adopted as the society's mascot. as a symbol of the sweet easy, simple times of the past. It was in 1809 that Pintard offered the following toast during the annual dinner parties: "To the memory of St. Nicholas. Let the noble behavior and behavior of our Dutch grandparents not be forgotten in the modern luxury and elegance of the current age."

The passionate remark about St. Nicholas that Pintard brought to the table at dinner were well-known to his friends and family. In the end, his family became bored with the subject and only had the means to indulge in a sluggish interest , and even humouring Pintard with half-hearted responses. Two of his closest friends were, however, still interested with the topic: New York-based author Washington Irving and Episcopalian minister and part-time wordsmith Clement Clark Moore.

Irving

Moore

The curious Irving first brought his attention to the saint in the beginning of January 1808. In that month, he wrote in Salamagundi an literary magazine of his own creation famous for its satirical portrayals of powerful politicians "The famous Saint. Nicholas - vulgarly called "Santa-Claus" - of all the saints of the calendar is (sic) the most revered by the real Hollanders and their naive descendents." This sarcasm flowing from this passage is a frequent theme in a variety of Irving's writings however, they are, in turn, laced with clues to his unspoken but true affection for winter. Irving made a second, more detailed mention of Santa Claus in his satirical historical work, History of New York. It was released with the Dutch pseudonym of "Diedrich Knickerbocker" on the 6th December, 1809, which is why the book was given an other title "Knickerbocker's History of New York from the beginning of the World to the end of the Dutch Dynasty."

In the History of New York, St. Nicholas was acknowledged as the patron saint of New Amsterdam and was described as an "jolly old Dutchman known as 'Sancte Claus". He drove his wagon up the roofs and then slid down chimneys carrying presents for children sleeping on the day of his feast."

To make sure that the celebrations were as good as the previous year's festivities The Pintard family asked an artist Alexander Anderson to produce a exquisitely detailed woodcut of St. Nicholas, which could later be handed out by guests attending the dinner party. Alexander completed the work the woodcut on December 6, on the 6th of December in 1810 Pintard excitedly displayed the woodcut with two panels.

On the left was a representation that depicted Nicholas who was a bishop depicted as a leathery-faced hairless, and haloed man with a white beard that was tangled with an ebony rod in one hand, and holding a large bag filled with gold coinage in another. The right-hand side of the image was two images of children and a girl who was well-kept with a lovely smile ("the good child") and crying boy sporting untucked clothing and sloppy clothing ("the the bad kid"). The two children were perched at the edge of a roaring fireplace, surrounded with two stockings. The text beneath these pictures said:

"St. Nicholas, my dear good friend!

Serving you for all time was my aim,

If you'd like give me something now, to give,

I'll be there for you all the time I'm here."

Two weeks later, in the same week, New York Spectator published a poem that praised the same "good saintly man." The piece of writing and the wooden cut had Easter eggs, which hints at the tradition's Dutch roots, like the oranges that were found in the stockings of a good-mannered child. This may be done to pay respect toward those who were the Orange-Nassau royals.

Pintard and Irving were able to turn St. Nicholas (and Sancte Claus) which was once a popular figure and an iconic name, however his connection to Christmas was not yet established. Christmas was a tradition within the New World since the colonial period, yet there was nothing religious about the festivities that were associated with it. The people wreaked havoc in the streets, and used the celebration as an excuse to drink barrels of liquor , and then drunkenly shoot out their revolvers.

Both Pintard as well as Irving both expressed their disapproval of this holiday that diverged from its original significance, numerous times. Pintard is the most prominent of them. He demanded that it be limited to the definition of a "family-oriented winter holiday that was appropriate for a gentle society." Irving parroted Pintard's views in his Sketch Book, published in 1819. When he described a family enjoying delicious Christmas dinner the author was advocating for the idea of a celebration that was family-friendly.

The Minister Clement Clark Moore was pleased with the rising recognition of St. Nicholas, but he was even more delighted to stumble upon an easy, yet unexplored route. The year was 1823 when Moore wrote "An account of the Visit by St. Nicholas," which was also published under "'Twas the Night before the Christmas Season." This charming verse, Moore purposely tied the appearance of St. Nicholas to Christmas Eve, hoping that it could further bolster the work that was the goal of Pintard as well as Irving.

According to legend, Moore found his inspiration while on an excursion to the shops in a sleigh. Moore created the character of Santa Claus on the character of a Dutchman who was from Chelsea.

"So all the way to the house-top the coursers that they flew.

With the sleigh filled with toys as well as St. Nicholas too.

Then it happened in a flash. I heard a rumble from the roof.

The pawing and prancing of every hoof.

While I was drawing my hand, I was turning,

The chimney is down St. Nicholas was able to walk with an unbound.

He was completely dressed of in fur. From his hair to his feet,

The clothes of his were stained with soot and ashes;

A box of toys was thrown onto his back

He looked like the peddler who had just opened his backpack.

His eyes were sparkling! his dimples, how sparkling!

His cheeks were as pretty as roses, and his nose was like the shape of a cherry!

His mouth, which was droll, was made into bows,

The beard on his cheeks was as white as the snow. ...."

St. Nicholas was no more a vindictive, glowering ghost in perpetually bad mood, but instead smiling, dimple-cheeked and red-nosed old man with beautiful, sparkling eyes. Moore's version of St. Nicholas was a kind and sweet-tempered, with the "round stomach that rattled like a bowl filled with jelly" and every note of his hilarious laughter. A number of other passages in the poem are detailed depictions of St. Nicholas' appearance as well as new details about his background were also revealed.

From the below, one can conclude from the following that St. Nicholas is a small man not much bigger than an elf

"But it was a miniature sleigh as well as eight tiny reindeer

With a very old-fashioned driver So lively and fast,

I knew instantly it was Saint Nick!"

They also revealed the names and genus of St. Nicholas' reindeer as well as the docking and landing methods were also revealed.

"...And the next thing I knew in a flash, I heard a rumbling on the roof.

The prancing and pawing every hoof...

He exclaimed and whistled, and named them:

'Now, Dasher! Now, Dancer! Right now, Prancer and Vixen!

On Comet! On, cupid! On, Donder and Blitzen!'"

In less than 20 years the poem by an anonymous author, which was free to be published in every newspaper during the wintertime, became well-known all over in the United States, and from there it was able to be a hit throughout the English world. "Genteel New Yorkers loved Moore's child-friendly, home-like version of Christmas like they were doing it throughout their lives."[55 Clement Clarke Moore took credit for the poem after, but some critics of literature believe that the original source was Henry Livingston, a farmer who wrote poetry that were published anonymously. Livingston's grown-up children later told him their father reading the poem to them as children.

In the years following, more writers were inspired to flesh out the story behind St. Nicholas. In 1849, the missionary and author James Rees published a short story called "A Christmas Legend," which added the character of Mrs. Claus to the mix for the first time. The plot centers around a lost couple who is able to knock on the door an uninvolved family and asks for shelter from the frigid winter weather. Near the close of the tale, the family realizes that the strangers - who they initially thought were Mr. as well as Mrs. Claus - were actually distant relatives disguised as.

The authors who were observant noted the favorable reaction to the new character, and a few of them immediately capitalized on the excitement. In the following years the Mrs. Claus became a recurring character in many books as well as poems and songs dedicated to St. Nicholas. The model Mrs. Claus was a memorable however, insignificant background character with a unique style and a love for festive Christmas parties. According to some reports the Mrs. Claus was accoutered in different shades of red, as in E.C. Gardner's essay "A Hickory Back-Log," she wowed the crowd in her plaid forest-green dress.

In the children's novel bestseller of 1878 Lill's Travels in Santa Claus Land and Other Stories and Other Stories, the character of Mr. Claus was portrayed as an affectionate wife and loyal secretary. The main character, Lill, describes her as "a woman sitting at her golden desk writing in a big volume." The husband and wife worked together as together and Santa telling the story of the children at opposite sides of the scope to wife who then recorded his observations in the notebook.

A painting from 1878 of Santa Claus and Mrs. Claus

A 1919 postcard featuring Santa Claus and Mrs. Claus

In the works of female writers Mrs. Claus was as kind and smart as she was outspoken and opinionated. According to Katharine Lee Bates' poem, "Goody Santa Claus on A Sleigh Ride," published in 1889 the Mrs. Claus demands to be permitted to ride on Santa's sleigh with the intent of delivering the gifts herself. She argues her case in the following paragraph:

"'Home to women is the best choice? Nonsense, Goodman! Let us eat our fruits!

Orchards provide the worth of women who are out in the open...

As I pull your fur cap a little tighter and kiss your cheeks with a ruddy kiss.

I'm so happy that I can sing, like sleigh bells go to bells!

Are you ready to put on your cloud-spun lap-robes? Tirra-lirra! Tuck me in."

Moore's Christmas poem became an instant hit and was so popular that newspapers across the nation reprinted it each time the holiday season were upon us.

Thomas Nast, a cartoonist and caricaturist for Harper's Weekly's retainer magazine, was fascinated by Moore's interpretation of St. Nicholas. Invigorated by the diverse yet compelling aspects in St. Nicholas' backstory that were floating around in the world of literature, Nast rolled up his sleeves and set to work to create an interpretation that reflected his own.

The first Nast Illustration depicting Santa Claus is published in 3 January 1863 issue of Harper's Weekly. The picture is politically charged that is with the caption "Santa Claus in Camp," the pro-Union, anti-Confederate Santa is dressed with a fur-trimmed jacket, which is decorated by white flags and patriotic stars, as well as striped pants that carry all the colours of the American flag. In front of Santa was a large crowd of soldiers in their adult years and one soldier is admiring the socks he was given.

Nast did not know that he was launching the beginning of a fresh chapter within Santa Claus' history in the United States. Santa's connections to the original Santa Claus had been snuffed out in favor of an unassuming character who promoted optimism, cheer and patriotism in the wintertime. There was rumors that the president Lincoln himself had engaged Nast to create the image for his recruitment purposes however, regardless of how it was done, the effect was evident in fact, Lincoln was so impressed with his results, he dubbed Santa "the greatest recruiting agent that the North has ever seen." On the other hand of the conflict the characters were used by parents to highlight the repressive power in the Union blockade "Not not even Santa could cross the dreadful Yankee blocking."

Nast ended up removing the obvious patriotic features in his later drawings that depicted Santa Claus. Santa's patriotic outfit was removed and his replacement was a simple coat and pants that were solid color as well as the furry top hat. Santa was not a spokesperson anymore for the Union and was instead was a kind father persona.

To be fair, kids across the globe have always been skeptical of whether or not there was Santa Claus, a conveniently obscure figure that was deeply involved in their behavior. Three years prior to the 19th century was to come to an end, one young girl decided to find out the truth to her own questions. In the first week of the month, the offices of New York Sun received a small, yet profound letter from eight-year-old Virginia O'Hanlon. The editorial writer who was the lead, Francis Pharcellus Church, was deeply moved by the request for information, and the letter and Church's reply was published on the 21st of September in 1897. The exchange would eventually be a record-breaker as the most frequently reprinted editorial ever.

The letter from O'Hanlon read:

"DEAR EDITOR:

I am eighteen years old. My little buddies believe that there is no Santa Claus. Papa says, "If you can see it in the SUN, it's true.'

Tell me the truth. Is there an actual Santa Claus?"

Church responded, "VIRGINIA, your little friends are not right. They've been influenced by the skepticism that comes from an uncertain age...Yes, VIRIGINIA, there is an Santa Claus. Santa Claus is real, as the love, generosity and devotion are present and you can be sure that they are abundant and bring your life the highest quality and beauty. Alas! What a miserable world if there wasn't Santa Claus. It would be as depressing as if there was no VIRGINIAS...Thank God he's alive and will live for ever. In a thousand years, Virginia, nay, 10 times ten thousand years from now, he'll continue to delight the joy of childhood. ..."

Chapter 4: Santa Goes Commercial

"They do not believe that Santa Claus is a visitor via the chimney. He is in into the center of your heart." -- Charles W. Howard, the founder of the Charles W. Howard Santa Claus School

For all who knew him businessman from Scotland James Edgar was the reincarnation of St. Nicholas himself. In 1878, just after he moved from Boston, Massachusetts, Edgar created from scratch an e-commerce store. The name was appropriately "Boston Store" however, it later changed its name to "Edgar's." It was not just was Edgar an extremely positive and humorous person who had a hilarious laughter, but anyone who encountered Edgar was, as they put it enjoyed his unrelenting generosity.

Contrary to the brutal employers that compelled their workers to do overtime with no compensation Boston Store was not one of them. Boston Store was open from the morning until evening just three times per week. In this way, employees were allowed to close down the store at the end of the day, four days per week, so that the remainder time they could spend with family. Edgar was also a man who had the customer's best interests in his heart. He let customers with lower incomes put a set amount of things on layaway and offered 4percent monthly interest on the amount they could pay to pay for the deposit. The generous Edgar was also an excellent neighbor who was dedicated to helping his neighbors. He often paid the medical bills of indigent children living in his town and kept his identity secret.

Most importantly, Edgar was a fun-loving and fun-loving character who loved children just as he loved dressing up. Photographs taken by relatives as well as published by local papers showcase him in a variety of costumes that range from George Washington to Uncle Sam. On special occasions, like this year's Fourth of July, he took a trip to the roof in the Boston Store and tossed pennies as well as other trinkets of a smaller size to the crowd of people who were jolly below.

Edgar dressed as clown

In the early years following the launch of Boston Store Boston Store, Edgar added an extra pop of colour during the holiday season, wearing his preferred clown costume. The self-made tradition continued up to 1890 when he came across the Nast's Santa Claus in an old issue of Harper's Weekly. The next day the man walked into town and hired a dressmaker to create Santa's outfit - as depicted in Nast's illustrations - and designed to fit his measurements. Edgar later remembered the thoughts that whirled around in his mind, stating, "I have never been in a position to comprehend why this great man lives in"the North Pole. He's far from home. He only gets to visit the children once each year. He must live nearer than them."

When the Santa costume was finished, Edgar returned downtown to take his costume. Then he drew and posted a post announcing an opportunity to meet and greet with Santa Claus at the Boston Store. When the time came, Edgar was astounded by the incredibly long crowd of children and parents waiting in line outside the entrance. Edgar is often referred to as the the first department stores Santa.

Jake Rossen of Mental Floss reported the results:"The concept of a live Santa was so fascinating that Edgar's store was visited from as far as New York and Rhode Island. The following year, stores across the United States had embraced the concept that helped increase sales and foot traffic. sales...Unlike the majority of his successors, Edgar never had a space to relax and unwind. He was always on the move, constantly looking for children so they could feel safe with Edgar."

In response to the popularity of the secular Santa that had seen something of a revival in recent years, charitable organisations also began adopting the fictional Santa as their representative. The inclusion of the powerful spokesmodel, they believed that it would inspire more people to give and encourage regular donors to make more donations.

The year was 1891. Salvation Army captain Joseph McFee led a program which was designed to provide the Christmas meal to 1,000 less fortunate citizens during the Christmas season and at no cost. While he was thinking of ways to fund the initiative, he began to think about his time as a seaman back in Liverpool. At the port of Stage Landing, McFee recollected the location of Simpson's Pot which was a huge iron kettle that was empty and took coins from the passers-by. Then, at the end of the week, the money were sorted out and distributed among those in need.

After that idea occurred to him, McFee purchased an iron kettle that was similar in size, and put it up at the Oakland Ferry Landing by San Francisco's Market Street. McFee's kettle, which is now referred to in the "Red Kettle" was a massive success which allowed McFee to beat his goal.

In 1897 in 1897, by 1897, Red Kettle tradition had traveled to the East Coast, particularly the Boston region. The month of December was when different branches of Salvation Army across the United States organized fundraising events that led to giving out 150,000 Christmas dinners. They also promoted goodwill by hiring Salvation Army also promoted goodwill by employing unemployed men and dressing them in Santa suits, and assigning them with soliciting donations through the streets.

A 1902 photograph of a man donating money to Volunteers for America while dressed as Santa

In 1929 the year 1929, captain William Wincapaw, a floatplane pilot from Maine began in 1929 the "Flying Santa" program. The planes dropped off gifts as well as care packages for keepers of lighthouses as well as people who live in areas that were similarly isolated on the coast in New England. The official website of the society, Friends of Flying Santa revealed the origins of the program in more specific terms: "...[I]t began on December 25, 1929 the day Captain Wincapawtook his plane with 12 packages that contained magazines, newspapers and coffee, as well as candy and other things. These were merely luxuries, but everyday necessities that could help make life on an island a little bearable...He flew to lighthouses throughout the Rockland area and delivered these small gifts for the families of the lighthouses. Unaware of how much his gesture of goodwill and Christmas cheer was appreciated, he returned into home and spent the remainder of the day with his family. ..."

It is believed that calling the Coca-Cola Company the father of the modern-day Santa Claus would be inaccurate. Actually they weren't the first drink company to include

Santa in their advertising campaigns. White Rock Beverages, which was founded from Waukesha, Wisconsin, bottled fresh spring water purportedly coming from the healing fount located near the native Potawatomi settlements. And on December 19th, 1915, White Rock used Santa to promote sales for its mineral waters for the very first time according to an advertisement in The San Francisco Examiner. In the image, Santa is shown in front of an engine, bringing presents into neatly lined White Rock boxes.

White Rock Santa White Rock Santa reappeared in The New York Herald on December 10 of 1916, this time, he was driving a plane filled with presents. In 1923 Santa Claus from the White Rock Santa was featured for the first time in a colour advertisement and this time, within the issue from December 12, 1923 of Life Magazine. In this image, Santa is sitting in a comfy armchair, examining the naughty or nice list. Bottles that contain White Rock water, White Rock ginger ale that is branded and whiskey are arranged in Santa's office.

The Coca-Cola Company cannot be credited for bringing about that Santa Claus known and loved by kids all over the globe today however, the company definitely contributed to introducing the modern image in the heads of millions of Americans across the nation. The company began to experiment in advertising featuring Santa in the 1920s, and appeared in a variety of advertisements printed by local newspapers, like The Saturday Evening Post. At that time the drink was labeled as a drink that was suitable only during summer season, however, the company wanted to alter this. Therefore, they added an appealing slogan for their latest marketing campaign "Thirst is a drink that knows no season."

The initial effort of the marketing team to highlight the original design of their mascot that was modeled on Thomas Nast's snuffy Santa failed to impress. Then Archie Lee, a D'Arcy Advertising Agency executive, laid out the specifications for the brand new Coca-Cola Santa A neat and athletic individual who also served as a symbol of good character. The year was 1931. Haddon Sundblom from Michigan, an illustrator, was brought to create Coca-Cola's brand new and improved Santa Claus. Sundblom was instructed to draw an authentic "Santa" rather than the typical department store Santa depicted in previous advertisements.

Sundblom selected the Clement Moore's Santa as the basis of his character as described in this 1927 piece published in The New York Times: " A standard Santa...appears at New York children. The height, weight, and stature are all almost identical as are the red clothing including the hood, those whiskers in white. The plethora of toysand ruddy cheeks, eyebrows with bushy noses and a cheeky paunchy appearance are essential elements of the makeup."

Sundblom also picked an actual model by collaborating with his best friend an old salesman Lou Prentiss. In the event that Prentiss died, Sundblom erected an image mirror in his studio , and utilized his own image as a reference for Santa's appearance.

The artist was inspired by everywhere the artist turned. The kids who are sitting around Santa in the paintings of Sundblom were modeled on his own children. A mutt in his later works was modelled after the gray poodle belonging to a local florist.

Sundblom's Santa was revealed in the winter issue of 1931 of The Saturday Evening Post, featuring a brand new slogan: "My Hat's Off to the Pause that refreshes." Coca-Cola's Santa continued to make frequent appearances in this newspaper along with The National Geographic, The New Yorker as well as The Ladies Home Journal. Sundblom's Santa was not just popular with the general public. it was believed to have boosted the sales of the company's winter season (formerly their lowest season) possibly two or three times.

As with Coca-Cola and other aspiring entrepreneurs across the nation have rushed to get the most of secular Santa model's huge popularity in the world of commerce. The year 1937 was when Charles Willis Howard, an established Parade-marcher and department store Santa who controlled Macy's parade and Macy's tour, decided that it was high time to improve the art of parade-marching. The following year, he created his own school, the Charles W. Howard Santa School in New York, which remains the oldest, and most prestigious of its kind. This unique institution that was called in CBS as "the Harvard of Santa Schools," did not earn the title or its prestigious fame over night. Howard was an experienced professional who took highest level of pleasure in his work. He was determined to create the most impressive Santas that the world has seen.

At the beginning, every pupil received an "Santa Kit" with eyebrows that were glued on and a beard made of elastic along with the correct makeup, and so on. The classes offered by the institution included the background of St. Nicholas and the secular Santa Claus as well as understanding the geographic geography surrounding Santa Claus's North Pole, as well as lectures designed to make students familiar with the reindeer, including live demonstrations. A separate curriculum was designed for those who wanted to be Mother Christmases. Tom Valent, the current director of the school (now located in Midland, Michigan), described Howard's primary purpose: "When you portray the image of Santa Claus It's an honor, it's an honour, and it's a amazing thing. It's about making people happy, and taking pleasure in the Christmas spirit that spirit Santa Claus. When you make people satisfied, you'll know what they feel, and they tell you how happy they are. It's a feeling that increases [and increasesand grows."

In the month of January 1939, management team of Montgomery Ward's Chicago headquarters at Montgomery Ward, a nationally famous retailer had a meeting and discussed ideas with the potential to drive their winter sales into the stratosphere. Prior to that the department store had sold coloring books with a Christmas theme to kids throughout the holiday season and was a highly profitable business model. It was discovered by one of the top executives however that it was more efficient and profitable to create a unique Christmas-themed coloring book on their own.

The copywriter Robert May was selected to be the person to take on the task. In the beginning, May found it difficult to overcome the obstacles in his creativity. He was in financial trouble and still battling the wounds caused by the Great Depression. The anxiety caused due to the growing tensions, a sign of the emergence of a major war in Europe and elsewhere, didn't ease his anxiety. In addition his wife was suffering from cancer, as well as the mounting medical costs of the insolvent May made his situation worse.

The task of writing a story that revolved around a cute semi-anthropomorphic animal May picked the traditional reindeer and named his protagonist with a red nose "Rudolph." As with many famous writers, May incorporated his own traits into Rudolph by describing him as a sly and misunderstood animal that was initially disregarded by his red-blinked nose However, his flaws eventually helped save the Christmas season. May was also influenced by the story lines of Moore's poem, as being inspired by his own Hans Christian Andersen classic, "The Ugly Duckling."

In December 1939 the 662 branches in Montgomery Ward presented to every children who visited a version of the 32-page fully illustrated pamphlet. This was nearly 2.4 million copies. A memo issued by the department's advertising department two months before provided the rationale of this strategy to market: "We believe that an exclusive story of this kind promoted in our newspaper advertisements and circulars will give every retailer an unimaginable amount of publicity...and even more importantly is a huge volume of Christmas traffic."

In the end, businesses of all sizes and kinds did not waste time getting the bandwagon. The years which followed Santa Claus merchandise was produced and then put out in mass quantities and included in boxes of cigarettes, chocolates calendars, bars of soap, and nearly everything else you could think of. Music of Father Christmas were also produced by the dozen, including "Santa Baby,"" "I I saw Mommy Kissing Santa Claus," "Here Comes Santa Claus," and "Santa Claus is Coming To Town." A secular Santa was also seen making a few appearances in commercials, praising "snow snow machines" the first day, and promoting Campbell's soup containers within the following day.

Another echo from the past, Santa's image was plastered across a number of propaganda posters that were distributed throughout in the United States during World War I and World War II. While the soldiers were fighting on the front, American women were expected to guard on the domestic front. The First Lady Eleanor Roosevelt urged women across the country to rise to the occasion and assume the positions that were left empty. The first lady told Americans, "A woman's place is in the factory, office market, courtroom and corner filling station and many other places to count." An article from 1941 in The St. Louis Star Times confirmed the logic of the words of the First Lady: "It [was] customary in times of war for women to assume various occupations normally reserved for males."

They argued they believed that women were not needed to perform the job of Santa. "There is a masculine domain...that must be protected at all cost," the author of the article stated. "A woman Santa Claus? Heaven forbid! It would stretch the credulity of innocent children."

Much to the dismay of conservative Santa purists, a lot of people have publicly supported the idea of female Santa Claus which included Charles Howard himself. In 1937 Howard announced the establishment of a female division within the Associated Press. The role that Mrs. Claus, said Howard was to "greet young girls, help them learn what they would like to find inside their Christmas stockings and help them play with dolls and dishware, doll homes and clothing."

Fortunately there were a few entrepreneurs who brushed off the outdated and gender-based norms at the time and set up an online platform to promote the first female Santa Claus. A caption under a photo that was published in the Associated Press in November 1942 describes the first time an department store owner who was a female Santa: "The manpower shortage is even affecting the old St. Nick...This female Santa Claus has turned up dressed as the traditional Mr. Claus except for the whiskers - in the Chicago department store. The kids seem equally content telling them what presents they're looking forward to."

Then, a month later, the Brooklyn Eagle reported, "Unable to locate a man who was suitable for the job the FW Woolworth store in Union New Jersey...also appointed a woman Santa ...[named Anna Michaelson, who was a Mrs. Anna Michaelson ...[Shehad on the skirt rather than trousers however, all other accessories will be identical to the classic Kris Kringle."

The phenomenon was met by a variety of reactions. Some were applauding the retailers for their innovative marketing technique, whereas othertraditionalists who were more sensitive were outraged by the new tactic at least to the extent that some, like the journalist Henry McLemore, were unable to perform. "[I was] shocked to the core in my entire life after I saw her].]... If there's such an thing as a minor terror, then the minor horror of this conflict can be women who are Santa Clauses. Kristine Kringle! Sarah St. Nicholas! Susie Santa Claus! "Holy Smoke!"

An article from November 1942 released by The Wichita Daily Times piled on the issue, claiming, "It may jar the young minds to hear a soprano voice rather than a basso deepo which is heard out of the whiskers." However the article ended with a shrewd conclusion: "[Children] have been sufficiently educated so far to pretend to not be aware that department-store Santa is a sham and to believe that the guile of a lady Santa does not put any unacceptably pressure on their pretended innocence."

A December 1942 piece published from The Washington Post may have summarized the situation in the most sensible position that could be taken: "Rather than disappoint the youngsters completely, it's more appropriate to have a female Santa instead of having a male Santa even."

Nowadays, Santa Claus is bigger and more widely known than ever before. There are countless mentions of Kris Kringle in books, films, poems, animations, films and other types of media and art in general, Santa Claus is commercially unstoppable. In 2016the retail industry in the United States alone saw an increase of 700,000 seasonal employment in the period of the holiday season. the same year, people have spent nearly $700 billion on Christmas-related shopping.

Department store Santas are now commonly called Mall Santas, continue to be highly sought-after with an average salary of between $35 and $50 per hour, or around $10,000 to $20,000. A portion of entrepreneurial Santa Clauses employed by small-sized employers and independent agencies make as much as $1,000 per day, providing entertainment at upscale celebrations and corporate gatherings of Russian famous oligarchs, celebrities and other notable people.

In light of the apparent longevity and worldwide appeal in the world of Santa Claus, one can only imagine what's in store Santa Claus in the coming years.

Chapter 5: Strange Adventures Of The Saint's

Body

St. Nicholas died in the year 842 He was laid to rest with great respect in the cathedral of Myra.

As Patron saint to such wandering populace as merchants, sailors and travelers , it is that his body would be in constant danger from the snares of thieves. Relics of saints were prized because they believed they were the benefactors of the people of the town and those who came to their shrines. Naturally the relics of such a famous and beloved saints such as Nicholas were particularly sought-after, and particularly by the class of people for whom Nicholas was his patron.

In those days of hardship when it was believed that nobody was particularly concerned about how his body was retrieved. Even if it was stolen and later reburied by the robbers the body did miracles in its new location in the same way it did in the former one. Additionally, it brought custom and trade to every city where it was buried and gave wealth to the inhabitants of the whole area.

In reality pilgrims from all parts of the globe gathered in great numbers to the shrine in Myra. The popularity of Saint Nicholas rose, as did the worth of his holy relics. In various instances during his first 6 centuries that followed his burial , attempts were made to take his body either through either force or through fraudulent means.

None of these efforts were successful until 1084, when merchants from Bari, a city of Bari in southeastern Italy came to Myra to find that the entire area was destroyed by an invasion by the Turks. The men who were able to carry arms had joined together and were in pursuit from the invaders. Three monks were kept behind to watch at the Saint Nicholas shrine. Nicholas.

It was easy for the merchants from Bari to defeat the monks. They broke the coffin that contained the body, and carry it to their home city.

It was welcomed with happiness. The church was built on the spot of the old one that was dedicating to saint Stephen and was taken down to make way for a new church. It was intended to be an altar for the body of the saint's stolen. The church still stands and is just as impressive as it was when it was constructed. In a vault or crypt underneath the altar are everything that was mortal to the Bishop who was once of Myra. The day before the reburial, it is believed that more than thirty people who attended the funeral ceremony were healed of various illnesses.

This is the tale that is widely accepted. However, another version was and is still being told by inhabitants of Venice. They also assert that they own the remains of Saint Nicholas and claim that it was stolen away from Myra in the year 1100 by Venetian merchants in 1100, and later buried at Venice by the people of Venice.

They don't believe in the tale told by Bari merchants. Bari merchants, but say they carried off from another location the remains of a saint, possibly with the same name, and they handed over to their neighbors as the remains of the Bishop who was formerly of Myra.

The actual body the body is believed to be located in the present, just as it has for many centuries within the Church in the church of St. Nicholas on the Lido. The Lido is an sand bank that is projected, in a prontory-like fashion out of the Grand Canal in Venice into the Adriatic Sea.

The popularity of a saint so closely linked to two major trading ports in early Middle Ages was sure to grow and spread to all countries of Europe. In fact everywhere, we can see that sailors recognized his role as their personal guide and protector, and were able to sing his praises everywhere they set foot.

Both at Bari and in Venice the churches named in his memory are located near the harbor's mouth. Venetian crews heading towards sea arrive on the Lido and then proceed toward the cathedral that is dedicated to St. Nicholas, there to request the blessing of their journey. Also, they would stop upon their return to offer gratitude for their safe return. Sailors from Bari were also expected to also pay respect to the shrine that lay what they claimed to be the remains of St. Nicholas.

Numerous stories about miraculous rescues from shipwrecks thanks to the help of their patrons, were told by seamen and travelers, not just at home, but also at the ports they stopped. Thus, the name and the fame of Saint Nicholas increased with each year.

The churches erected in his honour are everywhere in fishing villages and harbors in Europe.

The country of England alone, prior to the Reformation existed 376 church that bear his name. The largest church of a parish in the entire country is St. Nicholas at Yarmouth which was constructed in the 12th century and still bears the same name to this day. Other churches were re-baptized by Protestants.

The church dedicated to saint Nicholas within Catholic countries are particularly precious to those who make their living on the sea. Fishers and sailors who are on shore visit them. If they've just been rescued from any dangers of the sea, they express gratitude to their patrons by hanging on the walls of the church what are called votive images. They are usually images of the saint, or sketches sketched by the artists of local communities that depict the dangers the sailors faced and the way they had survived. A figure of Saint Nicholas is seen in the dark skies to soothe the fears of the beleaguered mariners.

It is the sailors and fishermen who play the largest role of the grand celebration in honour of Saint Nicholas which is celebrated in Bari on the fifth and sixth December each year.

Bari is, as it might be an interesting topic to discuss Bari is an ancient and significant seaport located on the coast to the east of southern Italy. It is located on a tiny peninsula that extends towards the Adriatic. Since its inception, it has been the official residence of the archbishop, and it has a cathedral that is grand and old.

The cathedral is magnificent, but as grand as it is however, it is surpassed in appearance and respect by its church dedicated to Saint Nicholas which I already written about as housing the remains of Saint Nicholas. The bones rest in the sepulcher, which is a huge tomb, which is located in a beautiful crypt twenty feet beneath the high altar.

The water gushes out of the rock that is the tomb. It is gathered by priests on a sponge snared to a reed. It is then squeezed into bottles and offered for sale or distribution under the name "Manna from Saint Nicholas" to treat for many ailments.

On the day before Saint Nicholas's Day, which falls on the day preceding the day of celebration (December 5th) Bari's city Bari is filled with a host of pilgrims from nearby towns, and those from the farthest regions of Italy and even Mediterranean France and Spain and Adriatic Austria. All Catholic mariners whose vessels are in port will surely join in the masses.

Staffs are that are decorated with palm, olive, and pine branches. On each staff is the water bottle, which will be filled with the Manna that is the gift of Saint Nicholas. The majority of pilgrims are walking barefoot. They all wear beautiful costumes worn at their homes during holidays.

As they enter the church, the visitors could, if they want to take a full circuit of the church, bending on their knees, with their foreheads being pressed time they step on the marble flooring. Most often, a small child guides them with strings or a handkerchief. One end is put by the mouths of the person who is walking.

The following day, December 6th, which is the actual celebration of Saint Nicholas is celebrated with an procession of sea-faring men from Bari. They get up at dawn and arrive at the church early to begin their day. Priests who are been gathered to welcome the guests, remove on the altar a wooden statue of Saint Nicholas who is dressed in the episcopal robes. It is given into the hands of paraders throughout the day. The priests are allowed to be present with the image, but only up to the outer entrance in the parish church. The procession, which has the image held in the hands of the leaders, marches out onto the street . It is followed by the people, visit the cathedral, as well as other sacred or public locations. The leaders then are taken by Saint Nicholas out into the sea on a boat. Numerous other ships can will accommodate the paraders and also people who can afford to spend the money and then follow Saint Nicholas through the seas.

The shore is also filled with the population of Bari and pilgrims who wait eagerly for their return to the statue at nightfall. Bonfires are burned as rockets are fired every person who owns candles or torchlights the fire and then the crowds fall into line with the paraders to return the sacred image to the guardianship of the church.

CHRIST-KRINKLE AND CHRIST-KINDLEIN

I've now shared with you all the details about Saint Nicholas in his lifetime, and even after his demise. I am sure you'll be able to agree that we haven't yet reached a great extent in making the distinction between Santa Claus, the modern Saint Nicholas and the saint of the same name who was once the Bishop of Myra.

True certain learned men have sought to find in the mythology of three girls, an answer to a few issues that trouble the curious mind.

In the beginning, they will explain the three gold-colored purses that, in paintings by the older Italian masters, depict in the form of three gold balls and were regarded as the sole symbol or representation of the saintly Saint Nicholas is the source of those three gold balls that are thrown over a pawnbroker's store in recognition of the source of human kindness that has earned him the popular name"uncle. "uncle."

If you've got an exceptional sense of humor, you'll realize that the last line is an expression of sarcasm. If you're a person with an interest in imaginative explanations that aren't clear why you should not, you'll be able to dismiss this idea of the origins of the pawnbroker's mark and will prefer to believe that it came from the gilt pills that adorned on the shields of the mighty Medici family from Italy. Medici means doctors. Both the name and shield are reminders of how the family gained their first fame as doctors several years before they became the most famous royals as well as the money changers in Europe.

What is the alternative theory? It's much more accurate. It is believed that saintly Saint Nicholas who was the Bishop of Myra is the Santa Claus of modern Christmas who he portrayed in the way he appeared during the evening and made important gifts for children.

Here's an appearance of fact. There is no doubt Santa Claus and Saint Nicholas are one in the identical. Today, our Christmas saint is referred to either Santa Klaus and/or Saint Nicholas, Claus in Dutch being "short and sweet" for Nicholas and as such it is similar to our Nick to Nicholas.

In the end it appears that there is very little in other ways in the relationship between the Saint of legend and the patron saint for the holiday season. What is the relationship between a charity event which is carried out at no particular date, and the amazing and generous nature that is Santa Claus, who every Christmas Eve, he fills his pockets with gifts for the little children he cherishes, and finds ways to distribute them throughout the world in one night?

If the answer isn't obvious from a distance Let us look at another legend. We will have to admit that the tale of three schoolboys who miraculously revived after having been cut up and salted , will not help us as much as the tale of three bags. It's one of a series of stories where Saint Nicholas is portrayed as the child's friend and patron. In this sense, only does the saint resemble us. Santa Claus.

In all the traits that modern storytellers and painters in America as well as in Holland and

Germany have conferred on the saintly and joyful of Christmas, he is quite different from the slim and even dehydrated Nicholas who is dressed in the clothes of a bishop wearing a mitre over his head and an emerald crozier in his hands which early painters loved portraying.

The legends about Saint Nicholas provide only a tiny hint as to the source of Santa Claus like Santa Claus, in fact, by name, however, he is different in all other ways.

Let's look our attention to another place. There is a problem in Germany in particular, and also to greater amount in America the term Christ-Krinkle, or Kriss-Kringle, is considered to be a different alternative to Santa Claus. But, as history has taught us, this is not the case as the two names have been joined in popular mythology.

A little knowledge of German can reveal that Christ-Krinkle refers to an "corruption" or a mispronunciation that is a mispronunciation of "Christ-Krinkle," which is the German term Christ Kindlein meaning in English refers to Christ child. The linkage between the Christ child and the Christmas season of giving gifts is evident enough. He is the Christmas hero day as a whole. Born as a human infant He has always maintained the love of children.

"Suffer small children to come to me," He declared, "for of such is the Kingdom in Heaven."

The masters of the past loved painting Jesus as a young child with children. In almost all of the famous images that Raphael one of the most famous Italian artists created in the form of The Holy Family or of the Madonna and Child The child Jesus is joined by the young Saint John as a playmate and friend.

.

The evolution of CHRISTMAS

At first glance it's difficult to understand why the Christ-child of the past, the Holy One whom we remember and celebrated in the feast that we call Christmas would gradually transform into the white-haired smiley-faced and warmhearted old pagan who we often refer to as Christ-Krinkle, but more often Santa Claus.

However, at the exact moment that we have to come with this thorny problem , we have come to the solution that was elusive as we attempted to understand the less shocking change of St. Nicholas Bishop of Myra and later Santa Claus, patron of the Christmas season.

We are reminded that the Christmas holiday that we have the present is a gradual development from the times that predated to the Christian period. We also remember that, even while it commemorates the biggest ever event during the entire history of Christendom but it was also based on pagan celebrations, and a lot of its customs are modifications of pagan ceremonies to Christian ritual.

This was not an accident. It was a necessity in a period when the new religion was imposing its beliefs on a deeply religious populace. To make it easier for new believers to the new religion and to make breaking old ties as easy as is possible These relics of pagan religion were preserved under altered models, much in the same manner that ancient columns, which were displaced to pagan temples, became part of the new church built by Christians to honor their God and the saints of God.

We can see that that when Pope Gregory appointed Saint Augustine as an ambassador to convert the Anglo-Saxon people of England, he instructed as that Saint Augustine to accept the unusual and unfamiliar Christian rituals with the traditional common heathen practices with which native people were used to since the time of their early days. For instance the Pope Gregory recommended to Saint Augustine to permit his new converts at certain feasts to feast and kill oxen to God's glory. God his Father for previously they did to honor the god of devils. The pagan gods, it is to be noted that they were regarded as devils among the first Christians.

After the Christmas of the arrival of his followers to England Saint Augustine Baptized thousands of converts , and allowed the traditional December celebrations under a new name, and with a new significance. He banned only the mixing with Christians with pagans and Christians in dances.

From these pagan-Christian traditions are the basis for several of the English traditions of Christmas that are still in use to this present.

Now, clear in your mind one important fact. While at the time that Augustine traveled to England the Christmas date was set as being on December 25, There is no reason in Scripture to support this. The gospels do not mention the time of year that Christ began his life. However they do mention that shepherds were at the time watching their flocks from outdoors. A lot of the priests and bishops believed that it likely that the Nativity occurred in the summertime or in the early autumn. It was a significant significance to them, since the Church of the beginning focused more on the day of death of a saintly or great person than his birthday. Birthdays are just the day on which a person dies and the day of his death is the day he was born into immortality.

The most important fact that led to the fixing of the date to December 25th was an agreement with paganism.

In the past, for a long time prior to the Christian period pagan Europe with all its diverse tribes and populations had observed their main festival around the time of winter's solstice, which is the time in the winter season, which has reached its peak and reached the point at which it has to slow down again to spring.

The final sentence needs more explanation.

The day with the shortest length during the entire year falls on on December 21st. This is also the day that winter is at its highest point.

It was on or around the 21st of December The ancient Greeks were celebrating what is now known to us today as Bacchanalia or festivities to honor of Bacchus the god of wine. At these events, people took part in dances, music, and other celebrations that often overstepped the boundaries of good taste and order.

In the past, in Rome the Saturnalia celebrations, or festivities to honor Saturn God of Time, started on the 17th of December, which continued through seven consecutive days. They also typically ended in chaos and disorder. This is why the terms Bacchanalia and Saturnalia were infamously referred to as "bad" in the later years.

We are particularly fascinated by the festivities of the old Teutonic (or German) tribes since they are the most closely connected to Christmas because we too are celebrating it.

The pagan celebration known as the Twelve Nights was religiously kept by them from the 25th of December until January 6th, with the last day being referred to, and is known to their descendants in the form of Twelfth Night. The Teutonic mind portrayed the forces of nature in their active form and imagined the living creatures as beings.

The battles between these forces were depicted as fights between giants and gods.

For instance, Winter was the Ice-giant, brutal violent, unruly the destroyer of all life and the adversary of Gods and mortals. While riding on his horse and the all-stiffening North Wind, he built his own castles made of frozen ice. Death and darkness came his way.

The Sun-god as well as the South Wind, symbols of life and light, offered the battle to the Ice-giant. Then Thor god of the Thunderstorm and flying on wings, unleashed his thunderbolt towards the winter castle and destroyed the structure. Then Freija goddess of flowers and fruits was back in her old sway. It's all a poetic way of saying after the Ice giant had defeated during winter, he took his own way overthrown by the Sun god in the spring.

The 21st day in December in the winter's deepest, was the time where the Ice-giant was at the full blaze of his victory. It was the day that marked the beginning of his victory. It was the pivotal moment in the struggle between natural forces. The Sun-god who had reached the point of the winter solstice was now seated on his fiery horses and became the sure signpost of the upcoming triumph of life and light over dark death of winter over spring.

There are a myriad of evidences to it being true that the Christmas season has integrated in itself the various festivals, Greek, Roman and German and has given these an entirely new significance. The wild celebrations of Bacchanalia and Saturnalia, Saturnalia as well as The Twelve Nights survive in a gentler form in the merriment and jollity that characterize the holiday season in the present.

Christmas gifts remind us of the present that were given out in Rome during Saturnalia. In Rome there was a possibility that, said that the presents typically included dolls and wax taperers, the former being an ancestor from the sacrifice of human beings made to Saturn.

It's a bit odd that with our Christmas presents we are also preserving in another style one of the more brutal traditions of our barbarian our ancestors!

The shrieks that rang out "Bona Saturnalia!" that the Roman people shared among themselves is the prelude to today's "Merry Christmas!" The Christmas decorations and lights at our Christian churches are reminiscent of that of the Temples of Saturn which were lit by burning tapers and adorned with garlands. Masks and mummeries that remain in use today including in the America of to-clay and that were especially popular during those of the Middle Ages, were prominent as well in Saturnalian celebrations.

A lot of the myths or superstitions, as well as the rituals that have risen up around the Christian celebrations across Europe as well as America are in some way exaggerated recollections of the legends, superstitions and rituals from the Twelve Nights of ancient Germany.

THEOR, SATURN, SILENUS

You might be tempted to ask "What significance is all this pagan celebrations on the issue as to the real identity of our dear Santa Claus? Santa Claus?

I'm getting there.

In each of these festivals , the main persona was an old man, sporting white beard and white hair that covered his face.

In Bacchanalia the god of Bacchanalia was not young Bacchus instead, the old cheerful, jolly, and definitely not-so-reputable Silenus, who was the main among the Satyrs and god of drunkards.

In Saturnalia It was Saturn an elegant and reverent old man, the God of Time.

In the Germanic feasts , it was Thor one of patriarchal origin and a warrior too.

The central persona of the Christian celebration was the child god--the Christ-Kindle, the influence of pagan long predecessors was too powerful in the heart of the new Christian world to be able to ignore.

The notion of hoary age as the real representative of the holiday season is a custom, as can be observed as a pagan tradition, on which all pagan nations were in agreement and still flourished beneath the rubble that were left by the old. It exploded once more after the past was considered too long ago to be viewed in a way that was disapproving or even provoking the Church. It was no longer apparent to be any risk of a repeat of the errors of religion of the past.

In the beginning, the more regal persona was selected because it was more appropriate for the solemnity of the time. Saturn was chosen over Silenus and was not consciously re-baptized as Saint Nicholas in the name of the most adored saint, whose feast was held in December, and who, in other ways, was the closest to being in line with the dark tradition that portrayed Saturn as the god for the Saturnalia.

It was long years ago that Saint Nicholas had ejected Christ-child from its first position in the Christmas celebrations. Indeed. He was often with his master on his Christmas tours. He is still doing so in certain countries in

Europe in which the modern spirit is the least evident.

As time passed when the concept of a worldly celebration during the Christmas season took precedence over the idea of thanksgiving and prayer The name Saint Nicholas became the most affectionate diminutive Santa Claus. With the new name, the saint who was once revered has lost all the austerity. He became more ruddier, jollier and more rubicund in appearance as the Christ-Kindlein faded further away from the scene, until the name of the former, under the slightly different name of Kris-Krinkle was given to his successor.

Then, look at the photos that depict Santa Claus which are scattered throughout this book with the ones of Silenus. Does it not seem obvious that there is a revival of the other? He has changed actually, with respect to certain characteristics of character, sucked up, cleansed and sanitized and dressed in warm clothes that are more appropriate for the cold season that the author has created his own, and yet God of the good people, the personification of good overall health and good humor, and happiness?

Extremes once again meet. The most modern hero of this festive season is returning to something that is old-fashioned. It is said that the Santa Claus of today is the Silenus of inexplicably ancient times.

Let's find out a bit on Silenus. Silenus was the tutor of Bacchus and appears to have had such respect for his student that his entire life after the discovery of wine was a lengthy trip. It was a fun and jolly affair however. Silenus was never a sourpuss or irritable in his drinks. Silenus was the most happy of drinkers. His attitude to life was as positive as his eyes. A smile of joy radiated over his huge, fat face. the light of humor glowed in his eyes that were ablaze with joy, his stomach was full of joy, and his smile radiated confidence of a relaxed attitude.

In spite of the many brute creations, the man chose an ass the caricature of a horse, as his most beloved charger. He was always accompanied by an entourage of satyrs and fauns who laughed all around him. His appearances were all the time the trigger for jokes and cranks as well as wreathed smiles.

Saint Nicholas in the past was known to travel the world with an ass. He still does in certain regions of Europe. In actual fact, all the wonderful characteristics of Silenus with the exception of drinking, are embodied by Santa Claus, the jolly pagan that is now the symbol of Christmas.

Although the modernized god of pagan worship holds this place in our festival the things that were offending in the traditional pagan tradition of celebration has been eliminated.

But it was not always this way. The Church, which had so wisely tried to preserve the ancient forms of heathens was often difficult, and often impossible, to conquer the spirit of heathens. Despite the protests from priests as well as the papal anathemas, even in the face of the criticism of all wise and noble people, Christians in the early days often replicated the most sinful vices and follies from the Bacchanalia and Saturnalia. Even the clergy were for a time plunged into the swirl. A particular celebration, known as "the Feast of Fools, was established in their name with the intention of ensuring the priests of the church that "the absurdity that we are accustomed to us and innate in us could be exhaled at least once per year." The intent was good. However, in reality, the freedom that was granted rapidly turned into a license.

The first time the Church's excesses, they were so significant that a council bishops that met at Auxerre was asked to look into the issue. Gerson was the most well-known theologian of the day caused a huge stir by stating "if every demon from hell had gathered their heads to create a feast that would completely smack of Christianity They could not have done better than this."

In the case that even clergy, pagan customs endured so vigorously how come they didn't survive in the lay community? The wild parties in the Christmas season in earlier times would bewilder the uninitiated. The amount of alcohol consumed and no act of blasphemy or obscenity was deemed unacceptable. The license was pushed to the limit of the law of licentiousness. Even in the 17th century, after the revelries were a little less raunchy master William Prynne discovered vestiges of paganism that are obvious to historians of the present.

"If we can compare" the sage states in his Histrio-Mastix "our Bacchanalian Christmas and New Year's tides" with these Saturnalia and celebrations of Janus we will see an incredibly close resemblance between them both in terms of timing, both being at the end of December, and the beginning of January. They also have a similar manner of solemnizing - both having been spent in revelry in epicurism, lust in idleness, dancing drinking, stage plays masques, sexual frolic that we have to conclude that the other to be merely the ape or the issue to the opposite."

The excesses that were a part of the Christmas season proved their own solution. In England The Puritans protested so strongly that for a period of time, they ended Christmas entirely. In Europe the change is more gradual. However, everywhere a shift in ethics and behavior has sanctified the celebration that Santa Claus presides, and Santa Claus himself, even when we see him as a rebirth of the pagan Silenus is actually an actual Silenus that is free of all the negative aspects of paganism. A Silenus who, thanks to his baptismal name change has adopted a brand new identity.

Santa Claus does not rule everywhere in the Christian world. There's even a massive distinction between Santa Claus and saints Nicholas who hails from Southern France and Germany. The Santa Claus of Germany, which is grave, sedate and severe and sombre, has more Saturn more than the Silenus kind. He is Saturn Christened and adorned with episcopal gowns. He gives out gifts just like Santa Claus, but in addition to giving gifts to kids who are good and carries a birch rod to punish bad kids. In the more primitive regions of the country, like parts of Lorraine as well as Bohemia, Tyrol, Bohemia and so on, he's accompanied by a demon called Ruprecht who guards those who are not good for girls and boys.

It's also a common tradition to observe Christmas Day for a couple or more maskers to dress in costumes of St. Nicholas and Ruprecht as well as other guests, like Christ the Child or St. Peter or who are not - these additional characters vary according to the location. They travel from house to house , rewarding children who are good and punishing those who are not so good.

There will be more on this to come in a subsequent chapter.

Chapter 6: Dangerous Christmas In Old France

In the history books as a symbol of the manners and behavior of the French court during the 14th century is a terrible incident that occurred in Paris on Christmas Eve of 1393. In the entire Christmas festivities that preceded it, riots was without a trace.

The wildest that were part of the French court were granted full reign. One outrageous prank after another until the imagination was exhausted from the process of inventing new tricks.

This was not the case with Sir Hugonin de Gisay. Sir Hugonin was regarded as the most crazy of the insane. The crazy and the ungodly enjoyed and admired him just in the same way that the godly and sober disdain and resent his. At the height of his position as a nobleman in the French court, he looked at with disdain "the common people"--tradesmen mechanics, labourers, and servants. He had a terrible delight in harassing innocent people like this on the public streets, poking these people with spurs whipping them with his whip and then directing them to walk onto their hands and feet in the sludge. "Bark, dog, bark!" the man would cry while the whip was whipped in the air.

To please him, the victims were required to bow as well as growl in the manner of dogs in front of the gentleman who was polite and nice allowed them to rise from their slumber.

On Christmas Eve on Christmas Eve, Sir Hugonin suggested that a mock wedding to be held between the two women who was a member of court. The proposal was greeted with cheers of joy. A couple of young people was selected to appear before a priest who appeared to be a real person, and then to perform the formal ceremony.

The ceremony was drawing to a close, As the ceremony was nearing its conclusion, Sir Hugonin requested the King and his four courtiers, who were madcaps for all of them, and all of them belonging to the most proud families in France and the world, to go from him for a short time. He had a new suggestion to present. Everyone in Paris was in a frenzy over the dancing bears that were brought into the capital by jolly performers. Hugonin's idea was that he, along with the king and four courtiers, would dress themselves as dancing bears. An eatable pot of tar as well as some tow were on hand to make them realistic bears that were in the booths of players. The courtiers then had to be joined by silk rope. The king would then take them to the hall.

"Excellent!" "Excellent!" cried the king, and all the courtiers with the exception of Sir Evan de Foix.

Sir Evan appears to have been the only member of the group who had the glimmer in commonsense.

He said that the group was about to be hurled into a room brimming with lights. Since they were all connected nobody could tell which disaster could not happen.

"Sire," he pleaded, "it is certain if one of us is caught on fire and spreads to the rest of us that is included, including your Majesty will be like a lot of the roast chestnuts."

Then came the insanity-filled Sir Hugonin. "Who would put us in flames?" He asked. "Where is the person who would not take care when the security of the monarch is at risk?"

Sir Evan's fears couldn't be put to the level of. However, when he realized that Sir Hugonin would prevail, he advised that at the very least appropriate precautions must be taken.

"Let His Majesty's Majesty's be forced on to at the very least give an order that no one with torch will approach us."

"That must be done immediately," said Charles. In a flash, he summoned the chief officer responsible for the hall, he instructed that all torch bearers must be brought in a single area of the room and in no way should anyone approach an armed group waiting to get in to dance. The orders being given the dancers walked in.

The crowd was greeted by a loud roar of cheers and laughter. The bears who mimicked them followed their leader through the hall, saluting women as they went by and swaying and dancing to the delight and amusement of everyone in the audience. "Who do they look like?" The spectators cried, eager to find out the identity.

At this time, The Duke of Orleans was seen at the entrance in the hallway. He had no idea about what was happening at the back of the room. He was joined by six torchbearers. They according to the rules, shouldn't have been allowed to the dance hall. However, The Duke of Orleans was the brother of the King. It was difficult for him to write to the prince of blood. He was not able to be included in any general arrangement. He was therefore able to enter the chamber.

"Who do they think are these people?" He yelled, reviving the sound that was echoing throughout the hall. "Well we'll soon discover."

In stealing the brand from one of his torchbearers, He looked into the faces of dancers, trying to determine them. Finally, when he came to Sir Evan de Fix, Sir Evan shouted his name and grabbed him with his arm. Sir Evan tried to free himself. But the Duke could not allow his grip to be released. Someone threw a jolt at his elbows, and the torch in his palm came into collision with the black twizzle that was used as bearskin. Within a short time, Sir Evan was glowing across the entire floor. In another, the whole knights were ablaze. Their furious fights served to bring them closer to each other within the silken rope they were bound by.

Luckily for the King, the king had gotten him out of the group after he been on his way to speak to duchess de Berri. At first, when the alarm went off, he would have been quick to assist his fellow passengers however, the duchess, thinking that it was the king in this disguise was able to wrap her arms around him and forcefully detained him.

"Sire," she said, "do you not see that your friends are dying, and there is nothing that could save you in the event that you were to come close to them in the dress you're wearing?"

In the meantime, one of the maskers had snatched himself free from his fellow maskers. The Young Lord Nantouillet known for his power, agility, and presence of mind. He was also the possessor in addition, a formidable jaw and a stunning tooth set. He chewed in the silken cord which trapped him, pulled off the rope, then ran through the hall before launching himself, like a fiery comet, through a glass which opened onto the backyard below. Fortunately, he remembered that under the window was the cistern that was brimming with water. After a plunge into the bathtub , he emerged burning, black and hot but he was saved.

For his fellows the group was now moving around in an uncontrollable crowd of spectators who were tripping over one another in their ferocity to avoid from the burning blaze.

Crying, praying, cursing, the four doomed men were battling with the fires as well as with each other. Women fell unconscious; and men who never failed in the most intense battles were nauseated by the horrific sight. While they were eager as they could be to help their fellow soldiers, they were well aware that no arm of a human could assist them.

All Paris was awakened by the tumult. Now, everyone crowds gathered around the gates of the palace. The flames finally went out. The four maskers layin in a scorched and writhing pile on flooring of the dance hall. One of them was nothing more than a tiny cinder. Another lasted until the dawn. Another one was dead at noon the following day. The fourth remained alive for three days of suffering. The culprit was Hugonin himself.

A shame that he did not learn from the tradesmen and mechanics of Paris!

"Bark, dog, bark!" was the chant with which they received the burned and mangled corpse after it was carried by the streets until it reached the final resting place at the graveyard.

The CHRISTMAS TREE IN LEGEND

We've observed that the majority of the events that were held or continue to take place during the Christmas season could be traced to an era long before Christ's birth. Christ.

The Christmas tree is not an exception to this principle. It is a pagan tree, and it is not Christian in its original form although it has been altered to Christian usages. It came into our culture from Pagan Teutons and Scandinavians and, along the way the cult was Christianized throughout Germany and Holland and Holland, as well as within Sweden, Norway and Denmark in the years before it had been sanctified in the same way as the English-speaking people.

The history and mythology have occupied themselves with speculations on the origins of mythology. Let's start with myth.

A long-standing legend claims saint Winfred the creator of the christmas tree. Winfred was among the first missionaries to Norway who worked to disperse the old Scandinavians away from pagan practices and beliefs.

He discovered they had priests who, called Druids were the ones who had taught that they should worship trees as like they were gods. Therefore, he took on the task of demonstrating to his Christian followers that the objects of their earlier worship were actually trees--trees , and nothing more. On Christmas Eve, he sawed down an enormous oak in the presence of a huge crowd of people, women and children.

Then, a miracle took place. It was, however, the result of a Christian miracle that made these people believe that their old beliefs were lost.

The miracle was described as such by an old historian:

"As the brilliant blade whirled around Winfred's head, the woodflakes spewed out of the deep gash that was forming inside the trunk that was the tree. A swirling breeze passed through the forest. It snatched the oak from its foundations. Then it fell backwards, as if it was a tower grumbling when it broke into four pieces. However, just behind it, not harmed by the destruction it was the young fir tree, which pointed an unfurling green spire toward the stars.

"Winfred let the axe fall and then turned to talk to the crowd.

" The tiny tree, a small kid of the woods will be your sacred tree until the night. It is the tree of peace, as your houses are constructed from wood of fir. It's a symbol of a life-long existence, since its leaves remain green. Look at how it points up towards heaven. This is the Christ-child's tree Gather around it, and not at the woods, but within your homes. There it will be a refuge for no acts from blood but love-filled offerings and rites of love.'"

There's another legend that is told by the inhabitants of Strasburg the famous city along the Rhine. Between this city and the nearby town of Drusenheim it is possible to see the remains of an old castle. It is believed to date back to the 7th century. Its most notable element is the huge gate. It is buried in the stone arch that is above the gate, with a sharp and clear outline as if it were made just a few days ago and is the mark of a delicate and small hand. This is the tale that is used to justify the presence that the hands are present.

One of the first castle lords was Count Otto von Gorgas. He was a dashing and attractive young man who loved huntering big game. In fact, so committed was he to deer shooting and spearing wild boars, that love could be unable to penetrate his heart. In vain could the most beautiful ladies in the land wait for a soft sigh or a gentle glance from this hunter. Mothers along both banks of the Rhine Rhine had given up in despair any hope of finding the huntsman as a suitable match for their daughters. Meanwhile, the girls themselves had gave him the name Stony-heart. This was how he was widely known across the country.

However the count Otto did not laugh at the fury of women, continuing to slaughter his own hands such huge amount of game that even new servants could not be brought to his service until he first agreed to offer them wild boar or venison steaks, not more often than four days during the week.

One Christmas Eve, Count Otto demanded that a battue or monster hunt to be conducted in the woods around his castle. The game was so thrilling that he was taken deep into the forest and, at night, was isolated from his fellow players and his followers. He remounted near an undiscovered spring that was clear and deep, and is known to the people of the countryside by the name of Fairy's Well. His hands were stained by the blood of wild animals he killed the previous day, he jumped off his horse and washed it off in the water.

Although temperatures were cold and white snow over the dead leaves, The Count Otto discovered to his delight the water from the well to be warm and inviting. The sensation of joy was felt throughout his veins. As he dipped his arms further into the water, he thought that his right hand was gripped by a different hand, which was more gentle and smaller than his and gently pulled from his fingers a gold ring that he had been accustomed to wearing.

When his hand was lifted out of the water , the rings were gone!

While he was upset by his loss, the count figured that the ring had slipped off his fingers. There was no chance for an additional search on this day, since the well was extremely deep and the sun already set.

Then, Otto remounted his horse and returned to the castle. He decided that the next morning he would be able to have an empty Fairy's Well emptied out by his employees. He was not in doubt, but the ring would be located at the lowest point.

In general in general, as a rule, Otto was a very good sleeper. The night he fell asleep, however, he was unable to sleep. In bed, he listened in awe to the hoarse roar of the watchdog in the courtyard until midnight. Then, he sat up over his shoulders. What was the strange sound that he heard outside?

He pulled his ears. Incredibly, he felt the sound of the drawbridge while it was being lower. In a few minutes, there were sounds that resembled the pounding of feet as they climbed the stone steps and into the chamber adjacent to his. Then , a wild swell of music floated in the air, sending the sweet, mysterious excitement deep into the "stony" hearts.

After waking up softly from his mattress, Otto hastily dressed himself. A bell went off. The door to his chamber was opened. He accepted what appeared to be an invitation that was not wordy. After crossing the threshold to the next room He was in an unintentionally small group of but stunningly beautiful strangers from both genders, who chatted, laughed and danced without even a single take notice of him.

In the center of the room was the most beautiful Christmas tree the which numerous lamps cast an enthralling light across the house.

This was the first Christmas tree that had that was ever observed in the region and by human being in any part of the globe. It was an evergreen Christmas tree of a kind that was never seen again by anyone across the globe.

In all likelihood, never will a Christmas tree bear these fruit. Instead of candy and toys the branches were decorated with diamond crosses and stars as well as jewelry made of pearls and aigrettes made of sapphires and rubies and baldricks with embroidered Oriental pearls and daggers set in gold and adorned with precious stones.

In awe of an event he couldn't comprehend, the count stared at the scene without uttering one word. Then there was a sudden movement towards the far end of the room. The dancers stopped and retreated to let in an unknown guest. In the bright light of Christmas lights, the most stunning vision appeared before the Count Otto.

The princess was of awe-inspiring beauty. While she was only a girl of size she was also an old woman. Even though she was petite her body was perfectly designed. Then she stood, exquisitely dressed in an elegant ball. A dazzling diadem glowed among her dark black locks. the lace of point only covered her bosom in snow and her dress made of pink silk was a perfect fit to her slim body with folds that were just enough to reveal the most elegant ankles and feet on the planet, and her sleeves were long enough to show gorgeous arms of sparkling whiteness.

The sweet stranger displayed no shyness or awkwardness. Instead after a brief pause, she ran straight to the count, grabbed the man with both hands and then said in the most sweet of voice:

"Dear Otto, I am waiting to take your phone."

Then she put her right hand towards his. In a bid to forget his previous negative attitude towards female sex, He smacked it with a kiss without saying anything else. He was indeed enthralled by the sight, awed. He was delighted to let the stunning stranger pull him to a couch , where she sat beside him. Her lips were in contact with his, and before he had time to think whether to kiss them he'd completed the gesture.

"My my dearest friend" said the woman to him "I are the fairies Ernestine. I've given you a Christmas gift. The present you lost and never expected to come across again, look! I bring it back for you."

Then, removing from her bosom , a tiny casket adorned with diamonds, she put it in the fingers of the count. When he opened itup, he discovered the ring was missing in the well of the forest.

Away by a sensation that was as bizarre as it was intoxicating, the Count Otto put his hand on the casket, and then the beautiful Ernestine to his chest.

"Delightful," murmured the maiden, and as you might have guessed, was not as coy like many maidens in the daytime world.

In short, the two were in love immediately upon first meeting. Prior to their separation in the evening, Otto had won the fairy's approval to be his wife.

The only thing she asked from him. He should not mention"death. "death" within her sight. Fairies are immortal. She would not like to be reminded of the fact that she was tied to an untimely husband.

It was not difficult to fulfill the promise and there was no doubt, he believed it would be simple to stick to it. On the next day, the next day, Count Otto von Gorgas and Ernestine who was the queen of Fairies were married in grand splendor and ceremony. They remained happily married for several years in the magnificent old castle.

A chance arose that the couple were to help at a huge tournament in the area. Horses owned by Lady Ernestine sat waiting to greet it at the castle gates. While she was busy adjusting her new headdress, which her milliner had brought to her home and she kept her husband in the waiting room until he had worn out.

"Fair dame,"" he squealed when she finally arrived in the hall, where for half an hour he had been jogging through the hall in his uncomfortable armor "you have been so long getting the right preparations, you'd be an ideal messenger to Death."

Just a few seconds after he said the fatal words, when with a shriek, the woman vanished. There was no trace left of her behind, save for the trace of her small hand at the castle's gates. On Christmas Eve but she returns and dances around the ruins with loud cries, and screams between each one:

"Death! Death! Death!"

For the count Otto, he followed the path of all flesh, and was brought to his father's soon after he lost his wife. Every Christmas Eve while his life was on for a while, he set up a tree that was lit in the room where he first encountered the lovely Ernestine and in the hopeless attempt to lure her back into his arms. This, according to the legends claimed in Strasburg and the surrounding area is the reason for the tree that is now a Christmas decoration.

THE CHRISTMAS TREE in the past

The stories I've recently told you might entertain you for half an hour or more. We must now move out of the realm of mythology to one of science and history.

My sexagenarian readers do not require an introduction to the field of study known as comparative mythology. But for the young ones, it could be beneficial to explain in as simple a manner as I am able to in just a few sentences the concept of comparative mythology. It is a type of human understanding that analyzes the myths and legends from one time and people to tales, myths, and stories from an earlier time and another group of people. The aim is to demonstrate how later myths are derived from older ones, or that each myth goes back to the same germ from the distant past.

With the help by the discipline of comparative mythology, let us look into the evolution of the notion that we see by the tree of Christmas. This led to a myriad of questions. Comparative mythology is among the most intriguing and challenging of science. It has to take into account the reality that we English natives in the present particularly Americans are a muddle-up mix of different races and different religions. In our brains, we have lingering memories of a myriad of conflicting stories from the past that, without being aware, we've inherited from our grandparents. In different parts of our brain , we keep the factual and fictional information that have been handed down in our lives by our parents or we've acquired from reading.

In every age and country We have evidence of the worship, in an earlier time of a tree as a god, or as the god.

The greatest and most well-known of these trees was an incredibly fictitious one, which is what Scandinavians called the Ash-tree Yggdrasil. No one had ever witnessed it, yet everyone among the people who believed in the existence of it.

It was believed to have a size that was so large that you couldn't even imagine it as a dream that covered the entire universe of the sun and moon and stars as well as earth. It also was said to have three roots, one in heaven one in hell, another in heaven and the third on earth.

The serpent that gnaws at in the roots of Yggdrasil is, in fact, an idea that was derived from the heathen world. But, you can't help finding a resemblance to the serpent in Genesis which is believed as a symbol of Satan or the Satan. Similar to Satan He seeks to bring down the whole that is the world.

If root of Yggdrasil are destroyed, the tree will fall and at the end of it everything will be over.

Today, in the Anglo-Saxons or the early inhabitants of England who were part descended from Scandinavians, Yggdrasil survived in the Yule log that was burned on Christmas Eve, and it still burns in the majority of English homes to this day.

And that's what happened when the tree of pagan origin changed to become what is now the Christian Yule tree.

The Anglo-Saxon missionaries have criticized their opponents of the Yggdrasil superstition. They had their converts cut to pieces all carvings that represented the idolatrous symbol and then they threw the pieces in the flames to show that Christ had destroyed heathenism.

In the case of Germans and among the Germans and Norsemen the sacredness to the Yggdrasil myth was not erased. It needed to be changed and adapted to Christian applications by linking it with Christian or Jewish symbolisms, like the Tree of Life from Genesis and the Cross of Christ found in the New Testament.

Examine the majestic trees Yggdrasil as well as its three branches to the description that

Alcima an author from in the beginning of Middle Ages, gives of the Tree of Life.

"Its place," says Alcima "is in a way that the upper part is in contact with the earth, while the root extends to hell and the branches reach across the entire earth."

Without doubt, Alcima was influenced Scandinavian mythology as well as biblical mythology. You can see that the meaning he used was not that of the real cross, but of it as an emblem for Christianity.

Let's extend our research by a bit further into the realm of mythology that is comparative.

There is a picture of Adam and Eve mentioned in older calendars, with the date the 24th of December. This is the day before Christmas. Our symbol for our parents' first Christmas are the trees of understanding of good and evil. Christmas is the celebration of Christ and its symbol is"the tree of Life", or the cross. It is evident that when people were moving away from paganism towards Christianity the tree from ancient mythology became connected with the birth of Christ and consequently with the cross. The light from Chanukah were incorporated into the lights of

Chanukah Festival of the Hebrews were incorporated into the tree of the holy as well as the candlestick with seven branches to represent the tree, was brought into churches.

The representation, which was so prevalent among early painters, and particularly the Italian painters--of the serpent sitting at the base of the cross was of course its Christian significance, but the adoption of this symbol to Christian art was to an important way affected by its significance that crosses had been commonly associated to the tree of serpents from the ancient pagan myth.

Scandinavia wasn't the only region to have the sacred trees. Egypt is one example. It was home to a palm tree which produces each month a new shoot. A sprig of this tree that had twelve shoots was utilized in the past of Egypt around the winter solstice, as symbolizing the twelve-month or the year that was completed.

From Egypt the custom spread to Rome which was included in the other rituals of the Saturnalia. Since palm trees aren't a thing in Italy Other trees were utilized in its place. A tiny fir tree or the top of a larger one was deemed to be the best due to its shape as a cone or pyramid. It was decorated with 12 burning tapers that were lit in the honor to the God of Time. The very top of the pyramid was the image of a radiant sun, which was placed there to honour of Apollo god of the sun who was the god of the sun, to whom three days that ended December were dedicated. The days were referred to as the sigil-aria, or seal-days because gifts were created from impressions carved on wax.

In further remembrance of Apollo whom was shepherd during his childhood, pictures of sheep were displayed grazing under the trees. Apollo himself would sometimes take responsibility for the flock or instructed shepherds on how to use the musical pipe. These customs were expertly modified by priests from the beginning of Church to Christian objectives. Shepherds and sheep were kept as symbols for Christ and his sheep. As you are aware, our Lord is often referred to as the shepherd of good repute and this is reflected in religious art. The sigil aria used by the ancient Romans was also adapted to a different purpose and the wax is now engraved with the images of saints as well as other holy individuals.

In the pages before, you read that the day before Christmas was the day that our religious grandparents dedicated for Adam as well as Eve. Therefore, you'll recall the first images of our parents were seen at the base of the tree. During the ceremony, serpents entangled themselves around the tree's trunk or roots. It was the serpent from the Old Testament, but I have already discussed how it was also an Christian version of the serpent from the great ash tree Yggdrasil.

The serpent makes its appearance at the bottom of the Christmas tree across many regions in rural Germany where traditional customs remain in their original form.

Prior to the arrival of Christ there was a swarm of people across the globe an belief of an illuminated tree represented holyness. It was that it was natural for it to be linked with the birthday celebration of Christ as well as the time that marks the solstice, which those who followed Christ were able to rescue from pagan practices and superstitions and had adapted to the faith that He founded. This connection was even more natural since the lights that twinkled at the top of Christmas trees were believed to be by the lighting of candles by the Jews on the occasion of their Chanukah (or Feast of Lights. Chanukah is celebrated by them in all its traditional ways. It falls on the twenty fifth day of Kislev the ninth month on the Jewish calendar. This roughly corresponds to the month of December, which is also known as the twelfth month.

That day, in the year 165 prior to Christ The temple of Jerusalem that had been profaned by the Roman military under Antiochus was cleansed and dedicated by Judas Maccabeus. Antiochus had lighted the seven branches of the candelabra which was continuously lit after the temple was completed. A sacred oil jar that was sealed with the ring of high priest, came to be found in a state of utter disrepair. It appeared to only be enough to last for a day, but when it was placed in the lamp, it lasted for a whole week. The miracle happened at the perfect moment as it would take seven days to get an additional supply of oil. It was later decided that the week starting on the twenty-fifth day Kislev was to be observed as a celebration for all time.

On that day every year, the Jews lighting candles in each home and the following day then two and so on until the seventh and final day of the celebration which is when seven candles light up every house.

If Christ had been born on the Twenty-Fifth day in December, it is likely that he was born in a period that every home within Bethlehem as well as Jerusalem was lit up with lights.

In this regard we can add it is believed that the German name to refer to Christmas can be described as Weinacht also known as Night of Dedication, as the idea that it was somehow linked in the popular imagination to the Jewish Chanukah. Another intriguing fact that points out the same idea is that the fact that Catholics from the Greek Church consider Christmas to be the Festival of Lights.

In addition, the Jewish celebration, Christmas shares an implied connection. It is the Passover in which the lamb is slaughtered and consumed. Christ is often represented by the image of a lamb. The saint John the Baptist You may recall that he was greeted by Jesus by calling him "the Lamb of God who removes from the earth's sins."

Chapter 7: The Christmas Tree In Europe

We are now considering the enigmatic roots of Christmas trees. We've decided that it's an adaptation of Yggdrasil as well as other holy trees from the past that were pagan to Christian and modern usages. However, we have not yet have we crossed the chasm that separates the past of the tree's old one from the one of the new.

What, where, and when was the Christmas tree as we know it was brought into the Christmas celebrations and affixed to the Christ-Child as well as Saint Nicholas? I'm sorry to say that it's not possible to definitively answer each or all of these queries.

There is a widespread German custom that makes Martin Luther the inventor of the fashionable Christmas tree. One Christmas Eve night, as Luther was on his way home in an icy country and was more than ever awed by the dazzling beauty of the night sky that was lit by stars above him.

It's a common phrase that is repeated by many intelligent men of the modern age it is that if a person had for all of his life been sleeping with the sun setting and woke up with the rising sun and therefore had never witnessed any moonlight or stars and suddenly woken at midnight, he'd feel overwhelmed at the dazzling beauty of the sky. People who have grown used to seeing the sky from our cribs can't be aware of the magnitude of such a shocking event. Since we've seen the moon and the stars for as long since we can remember, we don't realize how beautiful they look, and how stunning is the scenery they create. We accept them for granted, of routine.

Today, Martin Luther was a poet, as well as a preacher. One distinction between a poet and a person with a slower imagination is that his ability to bring an element of wisdom that comes from youth and innocence of childhood. He carries on the youthful heart but has the mature brain. Like Carlyle declared, he views the world "rimmed by wonder." Carlyle as similar to Martin Luther, a poet although he did not always wrote his thoughts in verse and rhyme, he never lost his sense that he was in awe and wonder at all the creations and manifestations of God throughout the universe.

God can be found everywhere but we, as a poor, sluggish people, only occasionally catch glimpses. If we could get rid of the haze that has gathered in our eyes throughout our travels through the world, we'd be able to see that God is everywhere. The poet is the one who keeps his eyes clean to see The Blessed Vision.

Luther returned home with a his mind and heart brimming with thoughts and feelings that had been triggered by the dazzling stars. He attempted to explain his family and his wife the thoughts and emotions were. Then a thought came to him. In the backyard, he chopped off the branches of a small pine tree and brought in the crib. He inserted candles into the branches and lit the candles. After that, Luther fixed up a Christmas tree at his house to teach and entertain of his family and his wife. The idea was replicated by his neighbours and then was adopted by all of Germany.

This is a wonderful tale, but it's an untruth and not a part of history. It doesn't deserve any more credit than the tale about St. Winfred which I have adapted from German folklore and the story of the fairy tale that is, as I've stated, continues to be a part of the lives of the inhabitants of and surrounding Strasburg.

It is believed that a tree lit with candles was used during the Middle Ages, and later as part of the Christmas celebrations.

The tree is believed to have played a role in a Christmas celebration held during the reign of Henry VIII in England. The tree is mentioned at an extensive length within the chronicles written at the period but it's evident that it did not have the most important characteristic of the present-day one. It was not the bearer of gifts.

As far as is possible to determine from the past the Christmas tree like we have it now, made its debut in Strasburg. This is significant since one of the earliest legends that explain the custom is found in the city. The most authentic proof is provided by an old document stored in a library in Friedberg, Germany, which was written by a Strasburg citizen of Strasburg in 1608. The text described an all-lighting Christmas tree adorned with candles and adorned with gifts as an annual feature of Christmas celebrations at the period. So, we can be sure the Christmas tree came to be a common sight in the area by the time of the 17th century. In addition, there is no guarantee.

The practice is believed to have taken root across Strasburg to the cities that lie on the Rhine and has thrived in this small district for over two hundred years.

In a flash, at the start at the beginning of Nineteenth Century, it made its debut outside of Rhenish towns, as well as other towns, and eventually took over the whole of Germany. In the next fifty years, it was able to conquer nearly all Christendom.

In 1825, in 1825, the English poet Samuel Taylor Coleridge, traveled to Germany to stay in the country. In one of the letters he in January of the following year mentions the Christmas tree being that was completely unheard of by his fellow citizens.

"There is a tradition of Christmas in the United States," he says, "which fascinated and amused me. The kids make little gifts for their parents and one another and give their kids presents. In the months of three to four months prior to Christmas, the girls are working and the boys are saving enough pocket money to purchase these gifts. The present to be kept a under wraps; the girls are able to come up with a variety of tricks to hide it, such as working even when they're away on trips, but those who aren't at home; getting up before the sun rises, and so on. In the evening on the day before Christmas one of the parlors is lit by children, into which parents are not allowed to leave; a huge yew-bough has been hung to the table just a few feet from the wall. A number of tiny tapers are hung from the tree however, not in a way to burn it until they're nearly gone, as colored papers,. is hung and flutters off the branches.

"Under this tree, children set out in a neat order the gifts they wish to give their parents. They also hide in their pockets the gifts they want to give each other. The parents then are presented, and each gives his own little present. They then take the remaining gifts each one at a time from their pockets and then present them with kisses and hugs. When I saw this scene there were around eight or nine children as well as the youngest daughter, and the mother wept in joy and tenderness and tears poured through his face. The father was in tears and he swung all of his children to his chest, it appeared as if he was doing it in order to stop the tears that was raging in it. I was deeply in awe. The silhouette of the bough, and its apex on the wall, and arcing across the ceiling created a beautiful picture and after that, the raptures of tiny ones, as finally the twigs and needles started to burn and the snap! It was an absolute delight for the kids!

"On the following morning (Christmas holiday day) in the large living room, parents lay out the gifts for their children. the scene of more solemn joy is created. As on today, mommy explains in private, to all her daughters, and the father's sons, what the father has observed as most admirable and sloppy when it comes to their behavior."

Continued, Coleridge tells us that earlier, and even in all the small towns and villages across North Germany, these presents were presented by all parents to young people who, dressed in high-quality buskins, white robes with a mask, an enormous flax wig , were the characters of Knecht Ruprecht. i.e. the servant of Rupert.

"On Christmas night, he walks all over the place and proclaims the fact that Jesus Christ, his Master was sent to him. The elder children and parents are greeted with great awe and respect While the infants are the most terrified. Then, he inquires about the children and, in accordance with the story is reported by parents, he presents them with the presents he planned to give them as if they had come from heaven by Jesus Christ, or if they had been poor children, he hands the parents a rod and by the name of the master, advises that they use it regularly. Around the age of seven to eight, children are invited into the secret and it's fascinating to observe what they do to maintain it."

THE CHRISTMAS TREE in ENGLAND and AMERICA

Coleridge's letter was composed on January 18, 1826. In the next month, the English people would be able to have an enlargement on the tree. An excellent German lady, Princess Lieven who had taken residence for a time in London brought numerous German traditions along.

"On the Christmas holiday," says Henry Greville in a hilarious gossip which was published shortly after the passing of Henry Greville, "the Princess Lieven got to throw a small party as is typical across Germany. Three trees, placed in large pots, were placed on the table, which was covered with pink linen. Each tree was lit with three tiers of circular wax candles:

blue, green white, red and blue. Around each tree were toys, gloves, pocket-handkerchiefs, workboxes, books and various articles--presents made to the owner of the tree. It was beautiful. It was a beautiful sight. the kids. The custom is now extended to all ages in Germany the custom is extended to people of all ages."

But, at no point did the custom transfer to England. People who had seen this tree at the parlor of Princess Lieven or who learned about it from people who had seen it, didn't make an effort to replicate it at home. The next 12 years would go by before the tree got solid root in English soil.

It was the union to Queen Victoria to an German Prince named Albert of Saxe Coburg that led to this outcome. First, the child of this union was an infant daughter (named Victoria after her mother) who was later crowned the Empress of Germany and was the mother of the current Emperor William. The second was a son, and is currently the King Edward VII of England. At the time Princess Victoria was just five years old, older, Prince Albert established an ornamental Christmas tree, German style within the nursery of King Edward VII in Windsor Castle.

A writer from the Cornhill Magazine identifies the date of the first introduction of Christmas trees in England in the month of December 1841. He recalls the time the parents of his "who were wintering in Germany and introduced it for the first time about 45 years ago, into England the awe it brought, and what awe-inspiring joy it brought."

The writer may give a bit too excessive praise to the parents of his. The mere existence of the queen would have made others follow their steps. The example of the queen was, however, sufficient. When a Christmas tree been installed in Windsor Castle, you may be certain that Christmas trees were lit and glittered throughout every British home who had the money to purchase one. It's remained exactly what it is for us: the center of all festive Christmas season.

The London News for December 1848 I've captured a photo that depicts what I believe to be the Windsor Castle Christmas tree with the English royal family of the time gathered around the tree. It's fascinating to observe the way this English newspaper handles the latest novelty that has come in from Germany.

"The tree chosen to celebrate this occasion," says the News, "is a young fir approximately eight feet tall, with six levels of branches. On each branch or tier are set 12 wax tapers. The branches that hang from them are exquisite bonbonnieres, trays, and baskets and other receptacles to store sweetmeats of the most diverse and costly varieties as well as of various forms as well as colors and degrees of elegance. Elegant cakes, gold gingerbread, and eggs stuffed with sweets are suspended with variously colored ribbons hanging from the branches. The tree, which is set on a table that is covered in damask white, is supported at the base by heaps of sweets that are larger in variety, as well as dolls and toys of various types, that are suited to young fancies, as well as the various ages of fascinating descendants of Royalty for whom they are presented. The names of all recipients is written on the bonbon, doll or any other gift intended for them in order that no difference of opinion about the selection of gifts can cause a disturbance to the peace of the famous children. At the top of the tree is a small angel-like figure with wings outstretched with each hand holding the wreath."

The tree was of interest for anyone who came to Windsor Castle from Christmas Eve the day it was first installed, and remained in place until the Twelfth Night, at which point it was removed. There were other trees set up in various rooms of the castle. Prince Albert was the one with his decorated tree that was presented by Queen Victoria who in turn was given a tree with the same style by her lady-in-waiting.

Two trees were also positioned on the sideboards in the dining area and were given, as we have been told, "a brilliant appearance when all the tapers are lit between these branches."

In America the Christmas tree had been an iconic feature long before it was introduced in England. German immigrants to the shores of America brought it along with them, much like in the past, the Dutch settlements in New York had brought over Santa Claus. It thrived in German settlements for a number of years until it was taken over by neighbors who were people who are northern descendants from the English Puritans as well as the Pilgrims and the Southern descendants of English Cavaliers.

New York, whose Dutch origins led to it leaning to the Teutonic spirit was the first place where German Christmas trees were first introduced. German Christmas tree found an appearance in a new location. The tradition gradually was adopted by people of different countries other than

German origin. Family fathers got into the tradition of a trip to the forest around New York to cut a young pine or fir tree to enjoy the Christmas season. If they were rich enough to have men-servants on their staff and butlers, they hired the butler or the footman to do this.

It is believed that a woodsman by the name of Mark Carr, who was born in the foothills of the Catskill Mountains in the early part of the 19th century was the first to create a business routine with Christmas trees. He was aware about the Christmas celebrations in the New York city. New York, where churches and private parlors were decked with hemlock and holly leaves. A tree of fir or pine was positioned in the middle of the nursery, adorned with gifts for children.

The young fir trees that were growing along the mountain sides in the vicinity of his country home could be used for this purpose. He would not take any major risk in attempting the idea. The only thing he would lose was the amount of time it took to cut the trees down and transport them to market, and the cost of several days' worth of life within New York.

Then, in December of 1851, the man began to put his plan in action. The month began when the two boys and he put together a couple of fantastic sleds, laden with young trees that were cut down from the nearby forests. After securing an oxen yoke to each sled, they drove them across the thick snow until they reached Catskill, which was on the Hudson River at Catskill, which is where his father began to take the sleds to the city.

One silver dollar was enough to secure access to a section of sidewalk at the corner of Greenwich and Vesey streets. The hopeful mountaineer set up his Christmas-themed forest novels for buyers. There was no time to wait. The crowds flocked to his stand. He was selling more trees for sale at more expensive and higher costs.

The following year, he returned to the same location with a bigger inventory and "from that point to the present," says Hexamer, an old historian from New York, "business has continued to be in operation until today. the hundreds of thousands of tree species are sold at Mark Carr's old corner."

In the present the Christmas tree cutters usually start their work around the first of November. They avoid early snowfalls, which can to create more difficulties for the company by melting, then freezing over the trees, making the branches too hard.

The pines and firs that grow in open areas are more attractive to those found in dense forests because they are larger and more symmetrical. After the trees are removed, the woodsmen stack them on the roads of the forest, which will remain healthy and green for weeks , or in the case of a need, for months.

The balsam-fir tree is the most popular Christmas tree in the eastern and middle states. The leaves keep their color and elasticity for longer than the black spruce of which a large portion is transported to market further to the south.

Chapter 8: The Story Of The Three Kings

Within the Latin states, Italy, the southernmost portion and the southernmost edge of France, Switzerland and Austria Our beloved friend Santa Claus rarely acts as the gift-giver during the time of Christmas. Even Russia even though it has chosen to adopt saint Nicholas as the patron saint of her country and has a celebration of his birthday according to her own customs does not give him a special role in the festivities which celebrate the birthday of Christ.

In all of these countries, it's not Christmas, but Epiphany Not December 25th however, it is January 6th which is the day in when presents are exchanged between family and friends.

Epiphany is most well-known among those who speak English as Twelfth Day is the day that celebrates The Three Kings, who figure in the New Testament story as the Magi or Wise Men of the East. You'll surely remember that the Wise Men were warned of the birth of Christ through the sight of a mysterious star in the sky, and then, following its instructions, they reached the stable at Bethlehem in which Jesus Christ was born.

They also brought gifts of gold, frankincense , and myrrh, which they gave to the Holy Child.

In memory of the kings who gave gifts that Epiphany was celebrated by the Latin as well as Russian communities is commonly regarded as the time to exchange gifts.

The Bible is silent within the New Testament about these wise men. The popular mythology has radically added to the Biblical tale. They are three wealthy as well as powerful rulers. Caspar the King of Tarsus in the merrh-soaked land; Melchior, King of Arabia in which the ground is reddish in gold and balthasar King of Saba in which frankincense gushes through the trees.

According to some writers they believed that these kings belonged to the bloodline of Balaam who was Balaam, the Old Testament prophet, who had prepared the gentiles to welcome Christ to the world. He had prophesied that an upcoming star in the sky beneath Judea. Judea and told his descendants that if they saw the stars, they should follow it and worship the great king who was to be born in Judea and become Lord of the entire Universe.

From the time of Balaam and Balaam, it is said that sentinels were posted on a mountain to the east in order that once the stars appeared in the sky they would be able to communicate this to the Lords and lords in the nation so that they could be quick to go and worship the new King. The announcement was, in fact was not required for Caspar, Melchior and Balthasar. As highly educated and wise monarchs, they were under guidance by Jesus Christ, the Holy Spirit who told them personally about the sign of the stars.

Every one of them simultaneously brought together a large group of servants, as in a group of camels, horses, and dromedaries, all filled with the finest products from their respective nations. They then set off seeking the baby King. They looked to the star for guidance as it moved ahead while they walked. they knew it was there to guide them in the right direction.

The exact location of the three kings' meeting isn't known, but they entered Jerusalem together. As they entered Jerusalem's gates, the star that had led them was gone.

The reason for this was line with the plan of God that upon the demise of their star-guide, the monarchs could make inquiries about the capital of Judea and through these means, they could announce the birth of Jesus Christ, the Son of God. Therefore, Herod as well as the Jews generally could have no reason to ignore the birth of Jesus, and "the dedication and care of the Magi will be a rebuke to their naiveté and indifference since they had Christ close by they didn't look for Him and these people were from far-off countries because of this reason alone."

The three Kings, as they walked around the city of Jerusalem as they rode through Jerusalem, asked every person they came across:

"Where are the remains of He who was made King of all the Jews? We've seen the star but have lost it."

They could not provide any details, since nobody in Jerusalem has seen the star.

One of the authors who wrote this tale stopped to applaud the "holy courage" that the Magi announced the new king of Jerusalem without worry of Herod who could have them put to death due to this reason. The writer cites with approval the words saint John Chrysostom uttered in his imagination to the King's.

"Tell me"Oh, good kings, do you be aware that anyone who proclaims an undisputed king during the reigning monarch is at risk of death and that you are doing this and put yourself in danger from Herod who could simply order that you be sentenced on death row?"

The writer cites with the same enthusiasm Saint John's response on his own query:

"The belief of those kings was impressive and the love they showed to the newborn King was so passionate and since they met Him, they were prepared to give up their lives in love for Him."

The story of how three mighty rulers with a massive army that included servants as well as beasts, had arrived in Jerusalem soon got the attention of the King Herod. He was very disturbed when he found out they were in search of a newly-born leader of the Jews who was well aware that Judea was not their kingdom. Judea was not part of his heirs through succession or birth, but rather he obtained the kingdom as an offer from Romans who had unlawfully acquired it.

The first step he made was call all the learned and wise men from Jerusalem and ask them which prophets told them concerning the arrival of Jesus the Messiah and the location where the Messiah will make his first appearance on the earth.

They replied that the baby was going to have a birth in Bethlehem He was even more upset. He immediately sent out agents to summon the King into his palace where he threw the kings with a lavish banquet. After the meal, the kings were advised to travel on to Bethlehem in the hope that they will meet the goal of their search.

"If you discover that the prophecy child has been born in that place," he added, "hasten return and share with me the good news that you also can be able to praise Him."

The kings pledged to perform as Herod asked, not aware of the deceit and guile that was brewing within his wicked heart. Then they continued their journey.

Just as they had stepped from the gates of Jerusalem then the star was seen again on the horizon. After that they arrived at the place that was where, 13 days prior to, Christ had been born.

There was a star that remained still, shining brighter than ever before in a way of saying,

"Here is He who you are looking for This is the palace for the newborn King. This is the heaven's court as the King's residence is."

Complex and strange must have be the emotions the wise people felt within their hearts when they were shown what the star had to offer them--this King's chamber who they were seeking was a space that was more suitable for beasts than men as it was not intended for human beings but rather for beasts, it had been created.

The stable's mother was looking over the manger in which was her divine Son. Her keen ear picked up the sounds of hoofs and footsteps beats from outside the gate. In sheer terror, she lifted the infant out from the manger and then surrounded him by her arms. This was the way that all three Kings, upon entering into the home, saw the mother and the child.

The scales fell away from their eyes. They realized there was no king of the human kind who was born in the world. It was rather the God of Heaven who took on his human body. They fell on their knees and, one at a time they walked towards him and praised the King of Heaven as God and as the Savior of mankind.

And then they presented Him with their gifts , which have now taken on an entirely new significance. Caspar's gold proved the babe was a king, Melchior's frankincense proved his status as God and Balthasar's myrrh served as an affirmation that he was man who was bound to suffer an unforgiving death.

Gold was stored in the treasuries of kings and frankincense was burned to worship God and myrrh was utilized to embalm the corpses of the deceased.

The baby Jesus received their gifts with gifts that were more valuable than ever. In exchange for gold, He offered the charity of God and spiritual wealth to incense, faith for myrrh, honesty and kindness.

In the night, the kings were warned by a vision they were not to return via Jerusalem as King Herod had a love of evil and lust for the baby Jesus and they were to return via other routes to their respective kingdoms. They obeyed with all humility and humility.

"From this came the practice that the church follows during procession, which is to leave the church on one route and returning via another. This is why it's ideal that everyone Christians should be taught by the Magi not just to find Christ however, after having discovered Him yet again, even if they lost Him and returned to Him in a different way than the other, because in the beginning, if they followed the path that led to sin, then they ought to return to the sinful ways by following the way of righteousness; and, in this nation they will reach the real country that is heaven."

When Herod discovered that the three kings had gone to their homes without fulfilling their promises to him, he was irritated. He issued an order directing children who were under the age of 2 years to be executed. He was hopeful that the Messiah would be slain along with the other. However according to it is written in the New Testament tells us, the Holy Family received a warning from the heavens and fled to Egypt prior to the agents of King Herod could get to their destination.

Regarding the three kings when they arrived, each in his capital city the three kings threw off their royal attire and renounced their royal status. They offered all their wealth to the less fortunate, and walked the streets proclaiming that the Messiah of mankind was birthed in Bethlehem.

7 years following the death of Christ on the cross, the wise men were discovered at India through Saint Thomas who, at first, was a skeptical disciple who had now been firmly in their faith also an apostle of the East. Saint Thomas Baptized them with the Holy Spirit, The Father as well as Jesus

Christ, the Son and also the Holy Ghost. they also became apostles of Jesus Christ. They were eventually as martyrs for their faith, and their remains were laid to rest outside the walls of Jerusalem.

Three hundred years went by. Then Saint Helena the mother of Emperor Constantine was the first to make her famous journey to Palestine. Although she was 80 years old, she was alive with vitality and energy. Her entire time and energy were devoted to the search of the earliest Christian remains. She was the one who made the discovery of the cross that Christ suffered as well as the tomb where He was burial.

She also discovered the grave of the Three Kings and carried their bodies to the grave with her when she returned to Constantinople in order to bury them inside the Church that is Saint Sophia. The remains were later transported to Milan before being moved to Cologne. They are displayed there in a chapel on the side inside the Cathedral resting in a golden relic, with their smiling skulls, adorned with gold crowns, their skeleton bodies covered in royal purple, adorned with precious stones of immense value.

It is the tale of The Three Kings as it is shared across Europe. Within the Latin countries and also in Russia the story is to be added that isn't known in other nations.

While traveling between Jerusalem to Bethlehem As this legend goes, three kings encountered an old lady who was cleaning her home.

She inquired about what they were planning to do. They told she they were on the journey to pay tribute to the King who was born today the Jews she begged that they would wait until she had completed her work. "I am willing to travel along with you" the woman pleaded "and be a part of your tribute."

"Nay," replied the King, "we have no time to waste. You must quit your job and join us."

The elderly woman was unable to leave her job until she was finished. When she did, it was too late. She tried to be king's wife, but they vanished from the eye.

Since that day, she has been walking all over the world looking for the infant Jesus. On the day of Epiphany she walks through the chimneys of homes, and leaves gifts for the infants like the kings did, leaving gifts to the baby Jesus and hopes with a glimmer of hope that she will discover Him whom she continues to search for.

The Befana is a popular figure in Italy she is referred to in the present in the present as Befana (a variant of Epiphany which is the Italian term for Epiphany) as well the Russians refer to her in Russia in Russia, she's known by the name of Baboushka or the little old lady.

On the day on the eve of Epiphany, Italian children carefully take out their pockets of clothesand hang them on the massive fireplaces, which are prevalent both in palaces as well as in hovels. At night, the Befana descends down the chimney, much as Santa Claus during Christmas Eve. If the children are good, she will fill their pockets with candies and other gifts, however when they've been bad, the only thing they get from her is charcoal and ashes, or Birch rods.

In Spain It isn't the Befana or the Baboushka and neither is it an individual of three Kings not less than Balthazar who is the bearer of gifts. On the day of Epiphany children put their boots and shoes in a safe spot close to the chimney and hope that Balthazar will take them in throughout the night.

From the beginning the character has been portrayed as the african blackamoor Negro. But this is not true from the beginning. In the drawings of Giotto or Fra Angelico, depicting The Adoration of the Magi Balthazar depicted as an unidentified white man. In the painting of Bernardo Luini, he appears with a woolly hairstyle with a black face and the big lips that resemble those of the Negro.

Between Fra Angelico as well as Bernardo Luini, Balthazar changed his appearance and changed into a color-blind gentleman.

In several Italian cities, it's the custom of shops in their shops to create a display of puppets believed to symbolize the three King's. The most prominent among these is the face of black Balthazar.

A TWO-TWELFTH NIGHT CUSTOMS

Twelfth Night, also called Epiphany is a holiday that is dedicated to Epiphany, the day of three Wise Men of the New Testament. They are the three kings from popular mythology. It is normal that one or more kings must be prominent during the celebrations of this holiday.

The entire trio is visible everywhere. For instance, in Milan, Italy, three young men are dressed in royal attire on Epiphany morning. They then mount horses in the same elegant attire as they appear at those gates. They are welcomed by large cheers, and then an elaborate procession begins. In the procession, there is an individual wearing a huge gold star is escorted by the citizens line up. Every corner, new crowds of people join the parade. They parade through the streets, eventually arriving at the cathedral. On its steps, the King's horses are removed, and they, together with their companions, march through the aisles towards the high altar where a statue of Christ the infant Christ is placed in the manger. Anyone who would like to can leave a gift to the baby Jesus in the manger. Then , the procession breaks up.

In Madrid there is a little playful joking can still be found on Epiphany Eve. Peasants from all over come to the city. They are often ignorant and religious. People in the town think that it's funny to gather in small groups, all performing on loud drums and thumping horns. The crowds march through the streets. They are thrilled to be a part of a ordinary person who is unfamiliar with the city life. A man like this is convinced that they are traveling for a meeting with the three royals who are likely to appear at the gate in the evening.

The mob calls on the citizen to join in. If he agrees and agrees, they put on an mule collar that has the bells strung to it around his neck. A step ladder is thrown into his hands. In the wake of the jingle of the bell he has set,, the unfortunate yokel is ordered to take the ladder and carry it through the streets. Every time he enters the city's gates the mob will stop and instruct that their victims climb the ladder, and then look up at the walls to check whether the kings are within sight.

When he gets to the top, they let him to fall, which could result in the danger of a fractured head or broken leg. If he is able to escape every danger, he's taken through the gates until faith or patience are exhausted.

In England in England, and in France only one King is crowned during the celebration of the Twelfth Cake.

France likely the original creator of this tasty called"the King's Cake, cherishes the tradition with particular fervor. Therefore, let's begin in Galette du Roi. Galette du Roi.

A cake's dimensions are determined by how many of guests to whom it is to serve. It is typically made of pastry and baked in an oval sheet similar to pie.

The bean was once baked into the cake however, nowadays, tiny china images are often substituted in place of the bean. Once the cake is ready, it's cut into slices , and the youngest child sitting at the table decides on how the slices will be handed out to the other kids. There is a lot of excitement as slices are handed out and consumed.

Finally, a person's teeth come in contact with the image and the person spits the image out. "He," I say on the assumption that it's an adult male. If indeed the case, then the name is"The King of the Bean (le Roi Favette) and picks one of the queens from among the girls. If it's female, she is named queen and chooses a boy to be her lover.

The queen and the king are constantly watched by their comrades. If either one drinks, the entire group must shout "The the king drink" (or "the queen drink," according to what could be. Any person who does not participate in the shout is required to pay a forfeit.

In England the customs vary depending on the location.

What happened in London at the beginning of the 19th century was best addressed by Hone as he wrote in Hone's "Table book:"

"First purchase an edible cake" according to this writer. "Next check the invitations on your list and count the number women you're expecting, and following that, count the number of gentlemen.

"Then you'll write on paper slips the names of all famous historical figures both male and female and then you write down the guests list. Each slip should be accompanied by an enjoyable line of poetry.

"Fold them in exactly the same size and numbers on each back making sure to mark the king's number. 1. and queen number. 2. Make coffee and tea be offered to your guests when they arrive. Once everyone has arrived and the tea has been served and the tea is served, place as many female characters in a reticule as are ladies in attendance; then place the male characters in a top hat. After that, you will need a man to take the reticule for the ladies in a row at a table. Each lady must draw one ticket, and keep it in a sealed state. Pick a lady to carry the hat for the gentlemen for the exact reason. There will be a ticket in the reticule and another inside the hat, the gentleman and lady who carried them both will swap, since they have been given to each. After that, you must arrange your guests in order of their numbers: the no. 1 king, the queen No. 1 The queen No. 2, and then on. The king then has to read the verse printed on his ticket, and the queen will read a verse from hers, and so on. the characters must follow in numeral order.

"This completed Let the cake and the refreshments flow around. And hey! to have fun!"

In the earlier times However, we are aware that cake played a greater role in the celebrations than Hone permits to it. Actually the English follow closely the French way of life that I previously described, but there was a time when in England the King's bean was complemented by an ounce of peas for the Queen. We can learn this from a poem written by Robert Herrick, who lived in the 17th century.

www.ingramcontent.com/pod-product-compliance
Lightning Source LLC
Chambersburg PA
CBHW050408120526
44590CB00015B/1885